You Can Say No to a Drink or a Drug

Susan Newman

Photographs by George Tiboni

A Perigee Book

> *The people photographed are acting. They agreed to play their assigned parts to help deliver the messages in this book.*

Perigee Books
are published by
The Putnam Publishing Group
200 Madison Avenue
New York, NY 10016

Book design by The Sarabande Press
Typeset by Fisher Composition, Inc.

Library of Congress Cataloging-in-Publication Data

Newman, Susan.
  You can say no to a drink or a drug.

  "A Perigee book."
  Summary: Shows preteens and young teenagers how to
resist or get out of difficult alcohol and drug-related
situations portrayed in ten photographically
illustrated scenarios.
  1. Youth—United States—Alcohol use—Prevention—
Juvenile literature. 2. Youth—United States—Drug
use—Prevention—Juvenile literature. [1. Alcohol.
2. Alcoholism. 3. Drug abuse] I. Tiboni, George, ill.
II. Title.
HV5135.N48 1986   362.2'92'0922   86-464
ISBN 0-399-51228-4 (pbk.)
ISBN 0-399-13222-8 (hc.)

Printed in the United States of America
    2   3   4   5   6   7   8   9   10

In memory of my mother . . .
and dedicated to young people
who want to be responsible
for themselves and their decisions.

You *Can* Say No
to a Drink or a Drug

Acknowledgments

In increasingly alarming numbers and at younger and younger ages, children are using alcohol and marijuana. I am grateful to those who accepted the magnitude of the problem and saw the need for the prevention information in this book.

Sincere thanks to Superintendent Gennaro Lepre for permitting me to select models from the Metuchen School System and to Fred Cohen, principal of Moss School who graciously expedited a lengthy list of requests.

Many people provided vital elements, be it their children for photography, their homes or facilities as locations, or their time. Of special note are John R. Novak, principal, Metuchen High School; Edward M. Joyce, principal, Edgar School; the First Aid Squad of Metuchen, New Jersey; Mayfair/Foodtown Supermarkets; Linda Graf, and Giulio Ferraro. Nina McGrath kept the details organized and the photography moving smoothly.

Meredith Varga and Kristin Muller, seventh-grade students, diligently offered suggestions to make sure that the book would be helpful to and understood by their elementary and junior high school peers. Putnam's editor Judy Linden expertly guided the manuscript to completion.

To Thomas G. Matro, assistant professor of English, Rutgers University, for his valuable criticism and to Alice Martell for her "agenting" talents and unwavering enthusiasm, a most appreciative thank-you.

Contents

You *Can* Say No
to a Drink or a Drug

You *Can* Say No

No matter who you are or where you live, chances are that alcohol and other drugs are within easy reach: in your parents' liquor cabinet, at a friend's house, in an acquaintance's pocket or purse, in a classmate's locker or backpack. Without much trouble you can get your hands on whatever drug you want—if you want it.

And, even if you don't want to drink or smoke marijuana, a friend, a group of friends, an older kid, perhaps your own brother or sister may try to convince you to join them. They may tell you that you don't know what you're missing: "When I'm drunk, I can do anything." "Stoned, well, everything is bright and cheery." They may call you a baby or a chicken. Or backward. A dork or jerk or worse.

Adults tell you that "It's okay to say no." But knowing it's okay to say "No" and saying it are two very different stories. Do you really want to say "No"? Do you know *why* you don't want to drink alcohol or smoke pot? Do you think you might like to try a drink? These questions need answering before you will be able to say "No" and mean it.

There's a good chance you will study about alcohol and other drugs in school. But what you learn doesn't always relate to what happens when you are out with friends, bored at home, or unhappy with the latest misery in your life. The stories in this book are about drinking and marijuana situations that you may find yourself in during the next few years. Perhaps you've been in similar ones already.

Neither your school nor your parents can be fully responsible for what you do. You're in this one alone . . . or should be. Most kids get into trouble with alcohol and other drugs because they really don't know how drugs work and how they change people—young or old. You'll see how alcohol and pot can cloud your brain and mess up your body.

You will also see how simple it is to start drinking and taking drugs. Each story will help you understand the pressure that may be on you. You are going to have to make some choices and some very difficult decisions.

All around you, adults and kids are drinking. Your parents may drink regularly at home. Some adults drink only at parties. You see adults drinking on television and in the movies, kids drinking on the sly. Alcohol looks harmless. Drinking looks like fun. It's supposed to. The one thing few people realize and even fewer tell you is that alcohol is a drug—a very powerful one.

Knowing that a glass of wine, a shot of liquor, and a can of beer each have about the same amount of alcohol or that if you drink long enough you will damage your liver won't stop many of us from drinking. But when facts like these are put with alternatives to drinking, with ways to handle unhappiness and pressure, and with an understanding of where attitudes about drinking come from, you will discover that drinking isn't what it's cracked up to be. You may very well want to hold off until you're older.

Avoiding drugs while you grow up is harder these days than it was when your parents were young. Then drugs weren't as close as homeroom or the shopping center. Your parents' friends weren't drinking and drugging out in the open and urging your mom or dad to break the law.

Today there also is enormous pressure from parents to act grown-up, to do well in school, to handle a divorce, to understand political bombings, and to stay away from drugs and be savvy about handling the opposite sex. You are expected to cope with all this by yourself.

The facts prove that young drinkers and drug abusers don't cope better with any of these problems. In fact, they stop growing up. The more they "use," the more immature they act. Saying "Yes" to alcohol and other drugs does the exact opposite of what most people want or think drugs can do for them.

No one can make you drink alcohol or smoke marijuana. No one can stop you. The decision is yours. It has to come from you. It's much easier to say "No" when you see that you can be popular, be a star, have fun, and that you can be part of a group *without* using alcohol, marijuana, or other drugs. You can say "No" and feel very good about that decision . . . and about yourself.

Chapter 2

Cornered

When Nancy called to say that she did not feel well enough to go to Ben's party, Liza was disappointed but decided to go alone. Since Ben lived two blocks away, Liza walked to his house.

Liza surveyed the playroom and saw many people she didn't know. Ben had told her that a few kids from their school were invited, but Liza recognized only Vicki, Rob, and Mark. And Benjamin, of course.

The music was so loud, Liza was astonished that she had not heard it at her house. She found Ben and warned him, "The neighbors are going to call the police if you don't lower the sound. How can your parents stand it?"

"Easy," Ben said, laughing, "they're away for the weekend."

"Oh." Liza didn't know what to say. She had never been to a party without an adult somewhere in the house. Her parents were not going to be happy about this. For a second she considered leaving but decided that would be acting like a child.

"Go get yourself a drink," Ben told her. "Over at the bar. Take whatever you want or ask Sammy. He's being our bartender. He mixes a great drink."

"Ben, you're drinking your parents' booze."

Ben lifted his glass and took a huge gulp of rye and ginger ale as a response. He giggled and walked over to a group of kids Liza had never seen before. Everyone had a beer can or a drink in hand except Rob and Mark. Liza felt as if she didn't belong. What did Ben think he was doing? she wondered.

She and Ben had been in the same class since kindergarten. They had played together and been friends even during the years she preferred to be with her girlfriends, and he, with his boyfriends. Most days they walked to school together. Now here was Ben being very loud and slapping people on the back like actors do in the movies. He looked silly to Liza.

This wasn't the tiny get-together Ben had told her he was having. Vicki wasn't a good friend of hers, but Liza went over to her anyway. "Hi, Vicki," she shouted over the noise.

"Great party isn't it?" Vicki smiled. "I didn't know you were coming, Liza. I didn't know who was coming. Ben told me his parents were away and he was having a party. You don't ask questions when the offer's that good. Know what I mean?" Vicki rolled her eyes.

Liza knew what she meant but didn't agree. Liza started to ask Vicki if there was any soda when some guy said hello to Vicki and placed a can of beer in Liza's hand. "Come on, Vicki, let's dance," he suggested. They walked to the other side of the room.

Liza started to feel very uncomfortable. She felt as if she didn't belong here and thought again about going home. Instead, she found her courage, put the beer can on a table, and went to the bar. "Sammy, that's your name, right?"

Sam nodded. "That's me. You name it, I mix it. What'll you have?"

"A Pepsi, please?" she asked.

Her "please" was muffled out by screaming and mimicking, "A Pepsi, please, a Pepsi, please, a Pepsi please," three guys repeated at the top of their lungs. Liza felt her cheeks go pink. She wanted to

disappear through the floor. They said it over and over, loudly, then in a high-pitched voice to try to sound like a girl. They stopped only to laugh. Liza froze, too nervous to move or cry.

The commotion they created was heard over the music and everyone turned to look in the direction of the bar. Ben came over to find out what was happening. Sammy teased her more, "Ben, you didn't tell me kids were invited to this party? This one, the cute little blonde," he said, pointing at Liza, "she wants a Pepsi. Can you stand it! Asking an important bartender like me for a simple Pepsi."

Ben thought Sam was terribly funny. Ben repeated Sam's words, "Can you stand it! Can you stand it!"

Liza pulled on his arm, "Ben—" she started but realized that Ben was not going to listen. She moved to leave, but was headed off by the boys who had been mocking her.

"Your Pepsi, madam," they said as they bowed like fancy waiters presenting her Pepsi in a tall glass on a small tray.

"Thank you," Liza answered weakly. She took her Pepsi, and they watched her until she took a sip. She coughed and gagged. There was something terrible tasting in her drink. Helplessly she looked around the room. The boys blocked the door. She wondered if they were going to stand there until she drank the entire glass. She'd never make it.

She needed Nancy. How could she have come here alone? she asked herself. Liza didn't know what the boys would do if she tried to get out the door. She could think of only one thing: She screamed, "Rob, Mark, where are you?" Liza surprised herself. Rob and Mark were two years older than she and Ben and they had never said anything other than "hi" to Liza, but at that moment they seemed her only hope.

"Drink your Pepsi, little girl," the boys insisted, "one more sip and it will start to taste good."

"Rob, Mark!" This time she shrieked.

"Liza, what's wrong?" Rob asked, seeing her cornered.

Rob took the "Pepsi" out of Liza's shaking hand and smelled the alcohol. "Stay with us," he told her.

The other boys sensed they had better back off. Everyone knew that Rob Young and Mark Merrick were the most popular boys in the area. They were smart, good athletes, and whatever they did, other kids tried to do but were never quite as successful. It was understood that you did not argue with them.

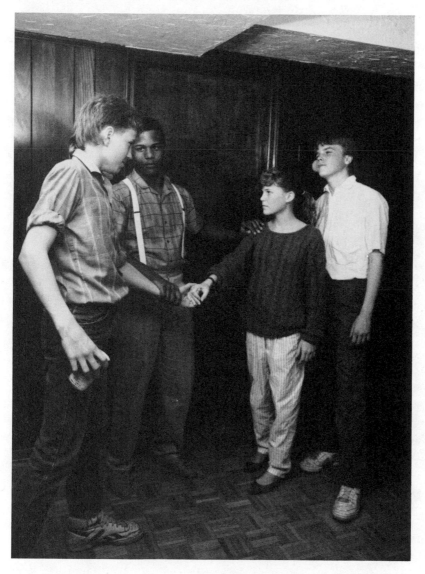

One of the boys was too drunk to care about Rob's and Mark's reputations. He approached slowly, trying to keep his legs steady. "Want to dance?" he asked Liza. He bobbed up and down like a broken jack-in-the-box, his eyes unable to focus on her face.

"No, thank you," Liza answered while looking to Rob and Mark for protection, which they gladly provided. "Stay with us. You don't have to drink if you don't want to," they told her. "We don't drink at these parties."

"How come you're always invited?" Liza wanted to know.

"I don't know." Rob didn't have a good answer.

"It's different for me," Liza said.

"No, it's not. Lots of the guys on the basketball team don't drink. They get invited. You'll get invited whether or not you drink. These guys were trying to be big shots, trying to get everyone to drink. It doesn't work that way," Rob continued.

"Don't you agree, Mark? Tell her."

"You have to do what you want, Liza. Want to dance?" Mark laughed, but his offer was serious.

"Thanks, Mark." As they danced, Liza promised herself that the next time she didn't feel right at a party she would leave immediately. She wasn't going to be pushed around or embarrassed again.

She and Mark danced one more dance. "This party is getting crazy," Rob announced, pointing to some guy about to "fly" off the railing. "I think we should get out of here, don't you, Mark?"

Mark agreed. "Rob and I will walk you home."

All the way home she could not believe how the evening had turned out. She had danced with Mark Merrick. Nancy would never believe it.

You Should Know

1. Most people don't realize that alcohol is a very powerful drug. Like cocaine, heroin, angel dust, and marijuana, alcohol alters how people think, feel, and act. That's why these drugs are called "mood-altering."

2. Almost every person expects to have a great time when he drinks. Some think alcohol will make them carefree or brave enough to say or try things they are otherwise afraid to do. Alcohol doesn't always work that way.

3. It affects people differently. Ben, normally a quiet guy, became loud and uncaring. Sometimes happy-go-lucky people become unhappy after drinking; others get nauseated and throw up.

4. Although alcohol is a food, it has no health value. Unlike most other foods, part of the alcohol goes immediately through the stomach walls into the bloodstream without being digested. Since a lot of blood travels to the brain, a person "feels" the effects of drinking within minutes. Unlike food, there is no "time delay" for digestion.

5. There's no predicting how a person will act as more and more alcohol gets into his body and brain. After the "up" feeling that comes from a small amount of alcohol, a person can become very depressed, get very sick, or begin to act in unusual ways: He may laugh uncontrollably, pick fights, hurt himself by banging his head against a wall, fall down steps from loss of muscle control, and say things he doesn't mean.

6. In a crowd such as the one at Ben's house, no one feels he must take the responsibility for what is happening. Each person believes he can blame someone else for starting the drinking.

7. Some people think that if girls drink heavily the way Vicki and others did at Ben's party they are "easy marks."

Keep in Mind

1. Your friends and acquaintances are your "peers." When peers tease you, shame you, or try to force or convince you to do something, they are putting pressure on you. This influence can be good or bad. It can help or harm you. It can make you feel terrific or terrible and guilty.

Talking a friend into drinking is being a bad influence. Talking a friend into trying out for a play he really wants to be in is being a good influence. Any type of influence—good or bad—a person uses, is called "peer pressure." We all know that peer pressure can be very, very strong. Dangerous peer pressure can be ignored or fought as Liza did.

2. People like Liza, who don't go along with the group, make those who are drinking nervous. They fear that the nondrinker is free to tell, will tell, and they will be in trouble. Because of this fear, they may increase the pressure.

3. Parties with no parent or appropriate adult in the house are trouble. News travels fast. A small gathering quickly can become a messy free-for-all with broken furniture, sick kids, and unpleasant scenes.

4. If no adult is visible, ask if one is present. A party is less likely to get out of control when a parent is home.

5. It's always a good idea to go to parties with a friend or friends who don't drink alcohol, smoke marijuana, or use any other drugs. Stay with nondrinking, nondrugging friends.

6. If drinks are being poured into glasses or paper cups, watch when yours is poured.

7. If you think someone has slipped alcohol into your drink, don't drink it. There's no law to prevent you from dumping the drink on the floor or in the closest plant if you're cornered as Liza was. Under other circumstances, pour a spiked drink in the kitchen or bathroom sink.

8. Leave immediately if you don't like what is going on or if you feel the slightest bit uncomfortable for whatever reason (you don't like one of the guests, you are unsure of what is happening in another room, people are drinking outside the house). It's okay to leave one minute after you arrive.

9. Tight spots like the one Liza was in are common. Ask for help. Look around for someone you know to help you or find a phone and call home. If the neighborhood is safe, waiting outside after you call for your ride may be less upsetting.

10. Liza took responsibility for her decision not to drink, knowing that she might lose Ben as a friend and might be called a sissy when the "word" got around. She survived rather nicely.

Chapter 3

The Big Split

Larry, Doug, and Chris, Doug's cousin from Cincinnati, rented bowling shoes and waited patiently for the leagues to finish. Lane number one generally cleared by 8:30.

While they waited, the boys told Chris how well they bowled, where they stood in the Future Pros League, and what fun they were going to have. At this, they both snickered knowingly as if they had some strange, devilish secret.

Larry and Doug were known around the bowling alley. They were there every Friday night. They had missed only two Fridays in the last two years, and that was because Doug had had the flu. He told his parents he felt fine, but there was no way they were letting him out of the house, especially since he slept at Larry's on Friday nights. They watched over Doug the way many parents hover over infants. For them, a runny nose or splinter was cause for concern.

"Hey, boys," Ken, the manager, called. "Lane number twenty-four is opening up. Want it? You're next."

"Great, let's go." Chris jumped up.

"No. We'll wait. Thanks anyway, Ken," Larry shouted over the clatter of bowling balls.

"What's the difference?" Chris wanted to know. "A lane's a lane."

"No, cousin," Doug answered sarcastically. "Wally and Jim aren't in lane number twenty-three or number twenty-five. They're in number two, and we want to be next to them."

Chris was puzzled by this explanation, but he was a guest so he kept his mouth shut.

"Okay, boys," Ken shouted, "it's all yours." The boys moved into lane number one.

"Hi, Doug," Jim greeted him with a beer.

"Thanks. We'll settle up with you later. Okay?" Doug asked puffing his chest slightly to impress his cousin. "Wally, Jim, this is my cousin Chris from Cincinnati."

Both men shook hands with Chris. "Want a beer?" they asked.

"Uh, no thanks. Thanks, anyway," Chris answered politely then whispered to his cousin, "Doug, your parents will kill you. You know they think drinking is a crime. Beer isn't even in your house."

"So what. Where you been, cousin? Everybody drinks beer. At least around here."

Larry, who had been listening, chimed in, "No beer in Cincinnati?" he teased as he took a foamy cup from its holder behind the seats. "You can get all the beer you want in my house. My dad will give it to you. Right, Doug?"

"Right. You too busy running around the silly track winning meets to drink?" Doug asked his cousin who was waiting to take a practice roll.

"That's not it at all. But drinking certainly won't help my speed."

"Beer makes me feel great. Chris, you should try it," Larry told him.

"It ruins your game. Even bowling," Chris offered.

"Naw," the boys responded. "Not ours. We do this every week."

Chris didn't feel like arguing. He smiled at Wally and picked up a bowling ball. "Who's going first?" he asked his cousin.

"You go. You're the guest," Larry suggested. He and Doug sat back and sipped their beers.

Chris rolled a strike. Larry and Doug looked at each other as if to say, "We're in trouble."

Doug threw a strike; Larry, a spare. The competition was building. The boys didn't speak. Larry and Doug did not like Chris's superior attitude. Without speaking to each other, they had decided that they were going to "whip" the Cincinnati cousin. In their determination, they drank faster than usual.

Whenever Jim got beer, he brought two extras for Larry and Doug. "Another one?" Chris asked each time, beginning to worry about going home to face his aunt and uncle.

"Sure, why not? I can drink six or eight like nothing," Doug boasted. "Hardly feel 'em. Bet we can drink Wally and Jim under the table."

"That's probably a bad idea," Chris said so quietly they had to ask him to repeat. "Nothing. I didn't say a thing."

A while later Wally asked, "Don't you boys think you've had enough?"

"We're having fun," Larry told him.

"No, just keep 'em coming," Doug mimicked one of those macho guys in television commercials. He strutted up to the balls and slipped, but recovered before anyone noticed his unsteadiness. Doug knew his cousin did not like what was going on. He and Larry had been having fun, but about three beers back, the fun had stopped for Doug. He rolled his ball down the alley and groaned as Larry laughed harshly behind him.

"The Big Split, Dougie boy. We'll never whip the Cincinnati cousin that way." Larry pointed at Doug to indicate the seven and ten pins that were left standing at the end of the alley.

Chris had felt out of it at first because he wasn't drinking, but now he was embarrassed. Doug and Larry were rolling gutter balls, bumping into each other, and laughing very loudly. Chris was wiping them off the scoreboard, but the competition had no meaning.

Chris was figuring out how to end the game when he saw Doug slump down on the seat. His face turned a sickly grayish white. "You don't look so—" Chris never finished his sentence.

"Looks like you overdid it tonight, Doug." Wally felt sorry for his young friend.

Doug stood up and swayed. Chris caught him and supported him to the men's room which, fortunately, was close to their lane. Doug threw up. He threw up again. Four times. Chris led him back to their alley, changed Doug's shoes, and put his bowling ball back into its case.

Larry joked and downed another beer.

"Come on, Larry. Change your shoes and pay those guys. Can't you see we have to get Doug out of here?" Chris told him.

"You know, you may be Doug's cousin, but you're a real jerk. Mr. Perfect, Mama's boy, won't have a beer."

"That's right," Chris answered, "I'm afraid of that stuff. Look at Doug. He's sick as a dog. Who needs it? He's going to have to get past his father, and I don't think you have any idea what that's like."

"I don't know and I don't want to. My father's easy. He drinks with me sometimes."

"What am I going to do?" Doug moaned. "I can't stay at your house. Chris is here."

Larry offered solutions. "We'll get you some mints. Comb your hair. Chris can say you had too much pizza."

"I'll cover for you this time, Doug."

"You will?" Doug asked gratefully.

"But you've got to cool it before your parents catch on."

"Mr. Preacher. Listen to him, will you?" Larry piped in.

Chris got tired of being polite and acting like a guest. "Come off it, Larry. That's enough. You think you're hot stuff. You're the jerk. Here, pay ours." Chris handed Larry his bowling shoes and money and led his cousin toward the front door.

The fresh air helped Doug some, but it was several blocks before he could talk. "Thanks for the help, Chris."

"Forget it."

"No, I can't. I'm really an idiot. I have to lie to my parents. I get sick. This isn't the first time. Maybe I'll bowl with Skip and Phil on Fridays. They don't drink. I could swim at the 'Y,' too. Bunch of guys in my class do that on Friday nights."

"Sounds good to me. You going to make it home?"

"Sure," Doug answered although he wasn't positive.

You Should Know

1. Larry and Doug drank a lot of beer before Doug got sick. People who drink on a regular basis—daily, twice a week, once a week—build up "tolerance." This means that it takes more and more of the same substance for them to begin to feel good, to get high . . . or sick.

2. Doug's dizziness, nausea, and vomiting most likely will continue into the next morning with the added ingredient of a pounding headache. These leftover symptoms are the well-known "hangover."

3. Drinking before or while participating in any sport—even bowling—can be very dangerous. Athletes who drink will find their endurance reduced and their balance greatly impaired. One drink can affect the part of the brain that controls coordination and movement. Drinkers have more accidents than nondrinkers.

4. Contrary to what most people believe, drinking before participating in cold-weather sports does not warm up a person. The skin may feel warmer, but alcohol actually lowers the body temperature. This lowered temperature can lead to a condition called "hypothermia," or dangerously low body temperature. Hypothermia can result in death.

5. Alcohol also dulls the skills—fast reactions, sharp vision, good judgment—needed to roll a strike, complete a pass to a "cutting" receiver, hit a jump shot, or ski down icy ski slopes. Like a drinker who drives a car, the downhill skier who drinks has a false sense of control and often takes unnecessary risks that lead to messy injuries and broken bones.

6. Swimming and boating safety are endangered when alcohol is consumed. One drink can put an excellent swimmer at risk. This happens because alcohol limits a drinker's muscle coordination, ability to regulate breathing and hold his breath, and ability to judge safe swimming distances. More than half of all drownings are the result of boat and swimming accidents in which alcohol was involved.

Keep in Mind

1. Bragging about how much he can drink (high tolerance) is a tip-off that the person may have or is developing a serious drinking problem or becoming dependent on alcohol.

2. Doug and Larry exaggerated their drinking capacities to impress Chris. This kind of boasting indicates that they are not the "big shots" they want others to think they are.

3. Doug drank heavily to rebel against his parents, who do not drink at all, who have no liquor in the house, and who think drinking is sinful. Whenever Doug has been out with the guys, after a party or a school function, his parents check his breath and stare in his eyes to see if they are bloodshot. On bowling nights Doug usually sleeps at Larry's to avoid his parents' inspection.

    Doug was angered by his parents' failure to trust him. But he was the one who suffered when he drank to get back at them.

4. Kids whose parents are morally against alcohol are likely to rebel by becoming heavy drinkers. It's a good idea to find out why parents feel the way they do about alcohol. The parent who is violently opposed to drinking may have a very good reason: an alcoholic parent, a parent who beat the children whenever she drank, a relative or friend who died from heavy drinking or was killed by a drunken driver.

    If Doug understood his parents' reasons, he might have been better able to bear their constant snooping and examination and less inclined to fight them silently by drinking.

5. Larry did not get sick because his tolerance is much higher than Doug's—with good reason. Larry drinks at home—a lot. He's accustomed to alcohol. His father approves; he believes drinking "separates the men from the boys." At first, that may sound as if Larry has it made, but boys like Larry are under a lot of pressure to prove they're macho.

Whenever Larry drinks he is proving to himself and to his father, even if his father is not around, that he's tough, that he's a man. This attitude and the quantities Larry drinks in his early teens make him a good candidate for alcoholism.

6. Parents who allow their kids to drink don't love them any more or any less than other parents. Often parents don't know how to stop their children, they don't understand that drinking is unhealthy or, like Larry's, they consider drinking a measure of strength and maturity.

7. Doug will be forced to lie if Chris can't sneak him past his parents. Lying, staying away from home more frequently, and borrowing or stealing money to buy beer are all parts of the pattern kids like Doug fall into if they keep drinking.

8. There's always a better way to spend time than drinking. Swimming on weekends is one of a zillion options. Start a list of choices: roller skating; ice skating; running; tennis; dancing; building model ships; playing chess, bridge, or backgammon; painting; designing pottery; weight lifting; or learning photography. You can probably come up with six more activities that do not need alcohol or pot to make them exciting or rewarding.

9. Whatever the selection, there's someone to join you. New surveys show that for every kid who thinks drinking is great, there is another one who disapproves. And antidrinkers—young and old—are increasing in numbers.

10. It's okay to admit that you're afraid, as Chris did. But if that's not your style, you'll see that there are many other ways to refuse a drink.

Chapter 4

So Stop Me

On Saturday Olivia and Joni were greeted by Scott and Amanda. "Hi, kids," Olivia said, smiling. "This is my friend Joni. Remember, she stopped by for a few minutes last Saturday? She's going to babysit with me today. Your mom said okay."

The children nodded shyly and turned to Olivia. "Can we go out? Just in the circle? We won't go past the yellow house."

"Sure. Your mom in the kitchen?" she asked Scott.

"Mom!" he screamed, "Olivia's here." Olivia zipped Amanda's jacket, while Scott pushed his sister's stroller out the door.

The girls went into the kitchen to get their instructions about feeding the kids lunch and what time to give Amanda her nap. Olivia hardly listened because she knew the routine. "Here's the number, if you have any problems," Mrs. Hartley said before she left for the afternoon.

Mrs. Hartley was Olivia's first choice for babysitting because Amanda and Scott could play outside without being watched every second and Olivia could drink. She smiled to herself as she thought about what a fun day she and Joni were going to have.

It was time Joni grew up, Olivia decided. I'm her friend. I'll help her. Olivia convinced herself that she was going to teach Joni a thing or two about drinking. She planned to show her how she rearranged the beer cans in the refrigerator so the missing ones would not be noticed.

Olivia considered herself very grown-up; she had been drinking beer for more than two years. Whenever her parents were out, she drank. Wherever she babysat she could usually down a couple of beers without getting caught. She would need extras for Joni, but in the Hartley's house that was no problem. Joni is going to love that buzz you get from beer, Olivia told herself. I'll show my friend.

Joni and Olivia settled in the living room. "Are you sure those kids can be out there by themselves?" Joni asked.

"It's fine. Mrs. Hartley does it. They were outside when she left, weren't they? If she didn't like it, she would have told me."

"Yeah, but—" Joni wasn't convinced. She kept looking out to make sure Scott and Amanda were fine.

"You know, Joni, you need to loosen up," Olivia told her friend. "You're uptight. You take everything so seriously. I have the solution for you. I know just what you need."

"What do I need?" Joni asked, not really convinced that Olivia had any useful suggestions. Olivia constantly picked on Joni and told her to change something: her hairstyle, her nail polish, the boy she liked, the dress she wanted to wear to a dance. Olivia found something to criticize about Joni practically every day. Joni sometimes thought Olivia was her mother. They both did an equal amount of picking. When Joni let herself think about it, she couldn't really understand why they did it. She didn't think she was that bad.

"You need a drink. That's what you need," Olivia said with authority.

"A what? Get serious, Olivia. I don't drink. That's the stupidest thing you ever said."

"I mean it. Drinking's great. Makes you feel good—happy. Come on, what do you say?"

"You're crazy. Where you going to get a drink anyway?"

"Here. There's tons of beer in the refrigerator. Come on, I'll show you."

Joni looked into the refrigerator and agreed that there was tons of beer in it, but she still didn't think what Olivia was doing was right. She watched her friend open a beer and start drinking it.

"Want one?" Olivia asked.

"No. What about the kids? How can you drink beer when you are supposed to be watching Amanda and Scott? What if you get drunk? What if they catch you? What if Mr. or Mrs. Hartley comes home early?" Joni's questions rushed out.

"Joni, you're such a baby. Take a sip then if you won't have your own." Olivia pushed the beer can toward her friend.

"Quick, come quick," Scott cried as he raced in, "Amanda fell down and she's crying and won't get up." Olivia hid the open beer can behind her back. Joni ran after Scott. Olivia stayed in the kitchen and finished the beer.

Joni bent down to see what was wrong, then picked up Amanda and looked her over carefully. She was bleeding a little on her knee, but otherwise she seemed unhurt. "You'll be okay, Amanda. Come on, I'll carry you inside and we'll clean you up."

Joni put Amanda on the table, washed her scrapes, and bandaged her knee. The three huddled around the patient who smiled, loving all the attention. "You smell funny. You smell like Daddy," Scott told Olivia.

"I do?" Olivia acted surprised. Joni stared at her. Joni didn't know if Olivia was upset, but she was.

Later, when Amanda was napping and Scott was watching television in his parents' bedroom, Olivia drank another beer which she kept hidden under a pillow on the couch. "You know, Olivia, if Amanda had gotten hurt, you would have been in deep trouble. An open beer. We weren't watching the kids. Doesn't that scare you?"

"You are such a baby. I don't know why I'm your friend."

"You really think I'll be grown-up if I drink a beer with you?" Joni asked seriously. "You'll like me better and stop picking on me?"

"No question about it. And you'll feel better, too," Olivia insisted as she sipped her beer.

"How many of those are you going to drink this afternoon?" Joni asked.

"Don't know. As many as I can sneak in," Olivia laughed.

"I don't feel right about it. My mom would have a fit."

Olivia laughed harder. "And mine wouldn't? She should only know."

"Know what, O? Tell me." Joni called Olivia "O" when they talked secretly.

"Forget it. You don't want to know." Olivia finished her beer and buried it in the bottom of the garbage with the other cans as she had been doing at the Hartley's for a year or more . . . ever since she started sitting for them on Saturday afternoons.

Joni followed her into the kitchen. "If you're taking another one, I'm going home. You can't get drunk while you babysit."

"So, stop me." Olivia put her hands on her hips and glared at Joni.

"Amanda could have been badly hurt."

"She wasn't." Olivia answered sharply.

Olivia had been sneaking a beer here, a beer there when she started. She knew Joni was right about drinking and taking care of kids, but she could not stop herself.

"Bye. I'm going home."

"You know, Joni, you're really not fun anymore."

Olivia told Mrs. Hartley that everything had been fine as usual, but Scott told his mother about Amanda's fall and how Joni had come outside to help. He also asked his mother why Olivia always smelled like Daddy smells when he watches football games.

"What an imagination you have!" Mrs. Hartley exclaimed to Scott.

While searching for a misplaced school permission slip, Mrs. Hartley figured out what Scott had been trying to say. She found four empty beer cans in the bottom of the garbage. She called Olivia's mother.

You Should Know

1. Kids who steal alcohol get caught. Sooner or later someone will discover that the contents in the bottle is disappearing, that cans of beer are missing.

2. Alcohol is habit-forming. Without knowing it, a person can become addicted. Addiction means that your body needs the alcohol to make it feel good. The urge to drink becomes stronger and stronger.

   Olivia's pattern of drinking—stealing at babysitting jobs, drinking at home—became a habit she could not control. Olivia needed help.

3. Some people are addicted instantly with their very first drink. It is believed that these people are biologically different. Hormones and genes are being studied to find the answer. Whatever the cause, the result is pretty much the same in alcoholics: The longing to drink becomes physical as well as mental.

4. Alcoholism in young teens develops more quickly and with less alcohol and fewer drinks than it seems to take in adults. Within one to three years a young drinker can become an alcoholic. Even if the signs that a person is drinking are not noticeable to others (as was the case with Olivia), *the disease* will be getting worse.

5. In over thirty-five states, minors can enter alcohol treatment and drug rehabilitation programs *without* parental consent and in some cases without parents having any knowledge that treatment is taking place.

6. More and more females are becoming alcoholics. Alcoholism is a disease that affects women as well as men.

7. Beer and wine are as addictive and harmful as scotch, rye, bourbon, and all the other "hard" liquors.

8. Although the alcoholic content is different in beer (4 to 5 percent), wine (12 to 14 percent), and hard liquor (35 to 50 percent), the standard serving of any one—one can of beer (12 ounces), a five-ounce glass of wine, or a standard mixed drink (gin and tonic, vodka

and orange juice, scotch and soda)—has the same amount of alcohol.

Without realizing it, by drinking beer Olivia was consuming as much alcohol as if she had been pouring her drinks from the Hartley's bourbon bottle.

9. As with attitudes about cigarette smoking, there was a time when people believed that alcohol was harmless. Today we know better. The long-term effects of drinking can be extremely damaging. The liver, which is the organ that works the hardest to break down alcohol so it can be eliminated from the body, can be damaged beyond its ability to repair itself even when all drinking stops. This condition, cirrhosis, often kills its victims.

Continual drinking can cause severe stomach pain and ulcers, brain damage, and lung or throat cancer. These are only some of the health problems created by heavy drinking.

10. Those who can't say "No" to alcohol and marijuana travel a dangerous road. In too many cases, drinking alcohol and smoking pot leads to the use of "harder," stronger drugs.

Keep in Mind

1. Learning to drink is not being an adult. Joni's assuming the responsibility for Amanda is an example of being an adult. Olivia was interested only in sneaking beer and getting high. This type of self-centered, juvenile behavior is very common in young drinkers.

2. Drinkers and pot smokers develop other behavior problems: They go from feeling great to being cranky, irritable, and unhappy very quickly. They have temper tantrums quite often. They switch friends frequently. They miss class and begin to fall behind in their schoolwork.

3. Young problem drinkers want company, especially when they understand what they are doing is illegal. In their minds, drinking becomes acceptable, even okay, if "everyone is doing it."

4. Don't let someone else decide what *you* should do. Olivia tried to decide for Joni. She tried to tell Joni that she needed to drink to grow up. Joni said "No" by walking away from the situation. A smart move.

5. Some teens have an easier time saying "No" when parents have established rules for them: places they may go, times they must be home, friends they may and may not see. Others promise parents that they will not drink. The majority, however, prefer to make independent decisions by following their own instincts and using their own common sense.

Chapter 5

Gone Too Far

"**O**ver here," Tom shouted.

Richie threw the basketball smoothly behind his back. Tom's jump shot swished through the net without touching the rim.

"Way to go," Hank cheered, tossing the ball to Greg. These guys were the core group. You could find them in the park playing basketball almost every afternoon. They had little else to do because they were too young for most summer jobs. After lounging around the house and hustling to meet the well-known requirement for play, they wandered over for the game.

Labor Day was in two weeks. By this point in summer, most kids in town knew the deal: Anyone could join the game if they "played" by the rules.

The National Basketball Association would have a lot of trouble with the entry requirement. The basic qualification was not as simple as it sounded: in order to get into the game you had to arrive at the park with a cold six-pack of beer. No one asked or cared how or where you got it.

Smitty was the primary supplier. His brother had graduated from college in June and was "legal." He saw nothing wrong with buying beer for Smitty and his friends every few days. This made Smitty a hero. Richie didn't have much trouble with the requirement because his parents were big party givers. Richie's folks had a refrigerator full of beer in the garage for the endless stream of company. On weekends, garage traffic resembled a parking lot before a rock concert. Richie's parents would never miss the beer he took.

The other boys had a harder time of it. Their sources were drying up. They had to hang out in front of liquor stores and supermarkets hoping someone would agree to buy beer for them.

They had long abandoned the six-pack rule, but outsiders didn't know this. Now they bought, borrowed, or stole as much as they could. Usually there was enough to turn the game into a show, which regulars in the park stopped to watch.

The boys were huddled in their secret, wooded corner of the park sipping beer. "I'm going to miss this," Tom announced seriously. "Just think, we'll have to go to class, study. I can hear my mother already, 'Tom, is your homework finished? You can't watch television. I don't care if Mr. Billings assigned the program.' She's such a pain about school."

"She can't be worse than my father," Richie said. "He acts as if I'm going to Yale next week. He demands—he doesn't ask— to see every paper. Not just test papers. Homework papers! I can't bear the lectures. My parents never let up: 'Now Richie do you know how important your education is . . . blah, blah, blah.' I don't think I'm up to it this year," Richie groaned.

"Stop complaining, you guys. Let's go play," Greg suggested, tossing the ball at Smitty. The others followed.

As they arrived at the court, Derek Walters, who was scouting his new hometown and park, got up the courage to introduce himself. He stopped Smitty. "How about a game?" he asked.

"Well," Smitty hedged, wondering where this guy came from, "not right now."

"Okay." Derek backed off the edge of the court. "I'll wait. I'm Derek Walters. We just moved here."

"I'm Smitty." After saying that, Smitty immediately turned his back and joined his friends.

Derek found some shade and watched. He could see that they were pretty good but they were clowning. The guy they called Hank dribbled the ball betewen his legs when he was unguarded; Smitty took long, wild jump shots when he could have driven to the basket. They often walked with the ball, but no one called it. Derek wondered if someone was going to drop out because it was so hot, but they played on.

Not one of them looked in Derek's direction. He felt silly and unwanted. When the whole group walked off the court and never glanced in his direction, he was positive they were ignoring him. It was clear to him that he wasn't going to make new friends today.

"Darn, we missed the game," Louisa pouted. She and her friend Ellen plopped themselves down next to Derek in what appeared to be the only piece of shade near the basketball court.

"You didn't miss much," Derek offered.

"Have they gone home?" Ellen asked.

"I don't know. They went over that way," Derek replied as he pointed to the woods.

"Oh, good. They'll be back then," Louisa said, brightening.

"Haven't seen you around here before." Ellen made a statement that was more a question.

"No, I just moved in. A couple days ago."

"Oh. I'm Ellen, and this is Louisa. Who are you?"

"Derek Walters. My parents bought the Cunninghams' house on Vineland Street."

"Judy Cunningham was a friend of ours. That means you'll be going to our school."

"I guess. I better get going." The conversation reminded Derek that he had promised to help his mother unpack.

"You can't go now. The best part of the game is coming up."

"How do you know that?" Derek asked.

"The later the better. These guys are so funny, you'll be rolling in the grass laughing."

"I watched them," Derek responded, "they weren't funny."

"They weren't drunk enough," Louisa giggled.

"What?"

"Drunk, bombed, out of their minds. Get it?"

"Sure I get it. But why would they want to play basketball drunk?"

"'Cause they do it every day. They have nothing better to do, I guess." Louisa noticed the puzzled expression on Derek's face and explained the requirement to him.

"Now I see. I didn't bring any beer so they won't let me play."

"You got it," Ellen sighed. "The whole thing is pretty stupid if you ask me."

"Why do you watch then?" Derek asked.

"It's on our way home. Louisa and I work for her dad at his nursery. Not a kids' nursery. Plants, flowers, shrubs. That kind. We do watering and potting, some planting. The easy stuff. On real hot days like today her dad lets us go home early."

"Ellen, tell the truth," Louisa said. "We watch because these guys are truly funny. Watching them is like watching a bad television comedy. The only thing that's missing is pie throwing."

"Lately, though," Ellen said, "they've been doing crazy stuff. They spray painted 'sick' words in the parking lot. When the park is crowded, I've seen Freddie and Smitty steal beer right out of people's coolers when they're down walking around the lake. Last week Hank and Tom dove in. That lake's gross. Ducks. Yuck. And their droppings. The park police have been watching them pretty carefully the last few days."

Louisa interrupted, "Here they come. Oops, Smitty is having a little trouble walking."

Hank bounced the ball off Tom's head. Tom faked a head injury and fell to the ground. The players huddled around him, picked him up, and roared with laughter. Only Greg seemed normal. They missed easy lay-ups; the game suddenly disintegrated to shoving and pushing. Derek heard Richie say, "Let's do something else."

Then Smitty shouted over, "Hey, you! What's your name? Want to play?"

"No, Smitty, he doesn't want to play. You guys can't even see the basket," Louisa answered for Derek.

Derek pretended he didn't hear the conversation. He needed friends, but these guys were out of his league. He couldn't drink like that.

Ellen made Derek feel better. "They're really good guys, especially Greg. I don't think he likes beer, but you know, those are his friends. You can play with them at school when they're sober. Oh, no. Look at them. They're bonkers today."

Tom and Smitty had climbed a tree and were trying to swing over to the next one. Hank was on the ground encouraging them. Greg screamed, "You're all nuts, get down!"

Richie thought so, too. He held up a can of beer. "Here's your beer. Come on down. That's dumb. You can't make it." They got rowdier and louder. People in other parts of the park were staring and walking their way.

Derek and the girls saw the police driving around the lake, fast. "This time they've gone too far," Ellen said. "Greg's mother is going to have forty fits."

"I guess the show's over," Derek sighed. "I'm going home. I'll see you at school." He had no intention of returning to the park. He didn't need these guys for friends.

You Should Know

1. Many, many kids like Hank and Tom drink to show off; some drink out of boredom. As Ellen points out, Greg clearly drank to be one of the boys. Whatever the reason, a lot of kids drink even when they hate the taste.

2. "Drunk" means having more alcohol in the body than it can burn off efficiently. It takes most people two hours to burn off the alcohol from one drink. Because the boys were guzzling beers, alcohol built up in their blood, and they became drunk.

3. A smaller person will react to alcohol faster than a larger one. Someone who is 5'10" and weighs 175 pounds has more mass and water to absorb and dilute the alcohol than does a person who is only 5'4" and 135 pounds. This explains why certain people will have trouble walking after a few drinks when others do not.

4. How a person reacts to alcohol depends on many factors other than size and weight: how much food is in his stomach, how much sleep he has had, his mood, his attitude about drinking, and his general health. The boy who has not eaten breakfast or lunch and stayed up until three in the morning watching a movie or TV can very easily become ill after one drink.

5. Four cans of beer for a boy weighing roughly between 150 and 160 pounds will increase his blood alcohol level to .10 percent. It's a good idea to know what can happen to the body as the level of alcohol in it rises. What follows is a broad summary.

- At .03 (one drink) relaxation, for some an "up" feeling of exhilaration, interference with coordination.

- At .05 (two drinks for most people), relaxation, slower reactions, reduced muscle control.

- At .10 slurred speech, limited muscle coordination causing unsteady walking, cloudy judgment, less self-restraint.

- At .20 difficulty walking, little control over emotions, sometimes confusion about where one is and what one is doing.

· At .30 and above unable to move, totally confused, difficulty breathing, unconsciousness, possible death.

6. Another piece of information everyone should have (not that anyone in his right mind would ever do this): A large amount of alcohol consumed very fast can kill you. Any kind of needling contest to prove who's the best drinker or who can get drunk the fastest may only prove who can get the sickest or the "deadest."

Alcohol depresses, or slows down, the body's systems. Adding a large dose of alcohol quickly can short-circuit brain signals to the heart and lungs, stopping heartbeat and breathing.

7. These boys are one example of the problem with most young people who drink: When they drink, they drink large amounts and become very drunk. In a drunken state they often get in trouble with the police.

8. Police can arrest and place minors on probation for a number of reasons: possession of alcohol; harming or destroying public or private property; physical fighting; disorderly conduct; any form of public disturbance; and harming themselves or others accidentally. One of many such incidents was the death of an old man who had a heart attack when drunk youngsters tormented him.

9. In a formal court hearing, juvenile courts can order young drinkers into rehabilitation programs.

Keep in Mind

1. There's one important difference between adult social drinking and kids' drinking. Many kids, by their own admission, drink for the sole purpose of getting drunk. Once they start, they don't usually drink one or two beers. They drink until they are intoxicated.

2. These boys began the summer drinking for the fun of it. But there's a good possibility that after a full summer of daily drinking one of them has a strong physical dependence on alcohol that eventually will turn into alcoholism.

3. The younger a person starts drinking the more likely he is to become an alcoholic. This is not simply a scare message; it's a pretty clear medical finding. An important growth and development gland—the hypothalmus—at the base of the brain is also a signal center. It receives messages and sends them to various parts of the body.

This gland is most unbalanced during preteen and teen years. "Attacking" it over and over with alcohol or other drugs can physically "hook" the young drinker.

4. Any smart person like Derek knows that a move to a new city, away from friends and familiar places; a parent's death, divorce, or remarriage; or any personal crisis such as the breakup of a long friendship, a horrible report card, or a canceled vacation can push him in the wrong direction.

The times a person is his loneliest and weakest are the times he needs to be the strongest and not use alcohol to solve his problem or make the situation better. Alcohol does not solve problems.

5. Any smart person also knows that alcohol is not a cure for boredom. The boredom trap can be avoided by planning ahead, especially for summer. Be a mother's helper (boys are as much in demand as girls). Offer to work at your mother's or father's office, store, or business. Help around the house with painting, yardwork, or gardening. Get a group together and form a company that will care for neighbors' lawns. Start a car-washing and -waxing service in your driveway.

Keep Out

"**H**ow come your brother hardly ever comes out of there?" Billy asked Ian as they considered sneaking into Kevin's bedroom.

"I don't know," Ian replied, shrugging his shoulders.

"Doesn't your mother get mad? If I'm in my room more than ten minutes, my mother's banging on the door saying, 'What are you doing? Come out of there. Keep me company. I need you . . .' Stuff like that," Billy explained.

"Mom did that to Kevin for a while, then she stopped when he started yelling at her to leave him alone. He locks himself in alone or with his friends. He mostly sleeps. He's a marathon sleeper. I stay in my room sometimes, but not every afternoon and every night.

"What really gets me mad," Ian continued, "is that Kevin's so mean to me. Sure, he's a senior and is going off to college, but he treats me like a baby or pretends I don't exist. I'm not allowed to set foot in his room. No one is. He doesn't let Dad or Mom in. They do whatever he says because they're afraid he will leave home if they don't. He doesn't play ball with me anymore. He's weird."

Billy felt that he understood because he had an older sister. Although Bev yelled at Billy a lot and had a fit if he went in her room when she wasn't around, she didn't keep her door locked and she joked with him and sided with him against their parents.

Bev was okay if you had to have a sister. "Is Kevin in there now?" Billy asked.

Ian shook his head. He could read Billy's mind. "He'll kill me if he finds out I've been in his room."

"How will he know?" Billy smiled.

"I guess he won't. Come on." They ignored the black and yellow KEEP OUT sign, slipped into Kevin's room, and closed the door.

Ian, who certainly got no awards for neatness, was overwhelmed by what he saw. "This makes my room look like a hospital. Wait 'til I tell Mom. Maybe she'll stop telling me my room needs cleaning."

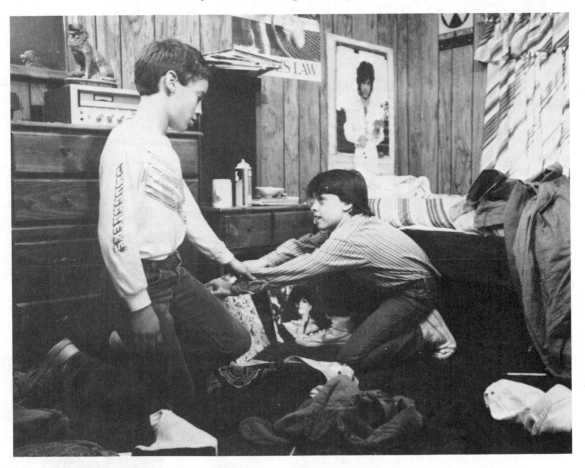

"Ian, you can't say a thing. We're not supposed to be in here, remember?" Billy reminded his friend.

"I forgot. Let's go." Ian pulled Billy's sleeve and moved in the direction of the door.

"Wait a minute. Let me look at Kevin's records." Billy began inspecting the collection. "Wow. I'm going to buy this one next time my grandmother gives me money for my birthday."

"This one's better," Ian told Billy. "I can hear it all over the house. Kevin plays his stereo so loud."

"What's this?" Billy put his hand in behind the records and pulled out a small plastic bag and held it out for Ian to see.

As they opened the bag, the bedroom door slammed back and Kevin yelled, "What do you think you're doing? I'll wring your necks!" Kevin charged the boys and grabbed the plastic bag in one hand, Ian's arm in the other. Billy watched.

"Calm down, Kevin. Let him go," Kevin's friend Patrick ordered and shut the bedroom door. "Let's be adult about this. You guys know what this is?" Patrick asked.

"Sure," Ian answered, "It's pot, and Mom is going to murder you if she finds out you have pot in your room."

"She's not going to find out," Kevin grabbed his brother's arm again.

"Stop it," Patrick said. The tone of his voice made Kevin release Ian. Patrick bent down and looked directly in the boys' eyes. "It's for older guys like us, but we're going to let you guys have some."

"You are?" Billy and Ian were surprised.

"Aren't we, Kevin?"

"I'm not so sure that's a good idea," Kevin answered, but Patrick had taken over.

"We are," Patrick told the younger boys, "but, Ian, you have to promise not to tell your parents. You too, Billy. Is it a deal?"

The boys didn't answer. They didn't know what to do or say. They were afraid to run out of the room, so they watched as Patrick rolled a joint. They were sorry they had gone into Kevin's room and even sorrier that they had been caught.

"How 'bout it, guys?" Patrick asked as he lit the joint. He took a drag and passed it over to Kevin. Ian watched his brother carefully.

Ian looked up to Kevin. He was the younger boy's idol. If I smoke with Kevin, Ian told himself, maybe he'll stop calling me a baby. Maybe he'll take me to the movies and drive me to school like he did last year. Maybe he'll be my friend and be nice to me like he used to, but Ian was afraid of his parents.

For months he had been hearing his mother and father complain about Kevin. They had accepted the business about not going into his room, but they were not buying his attitude or grades. He was failing two subjects and dropped off the debate team. One or the other of them yelled at him during dinner nightly, but Kevin sat there and looked at them as if they were crazy. A few times Ian had cried. He couldn't stand the yelling. He didn't want to be in the kind of trouble Kevin was in; he didn't want to be in any trouble.

In addition to knowing he shouldn't be doing it, Ian had another real problem with smoking pot: his mother would figure out what he had done. Sometimes she knew he was going to do something wrong or forbidden before he did it. Once he and Billy had planned to go to a rock concert, but told their parents they were going to the movies. As they were leaving, Ian's mother said, "I'll let you go this time, but next time, don't lie to me." Ian never discovered how she knew. This was the same kind of thing: She would know. She would just look at him and know.

Kevin interrupted his brother's thoughts. "What do you say, baby brother?"

"Leave me alone. I'm not a baby. What's so 'big deal' about pot anyway?"

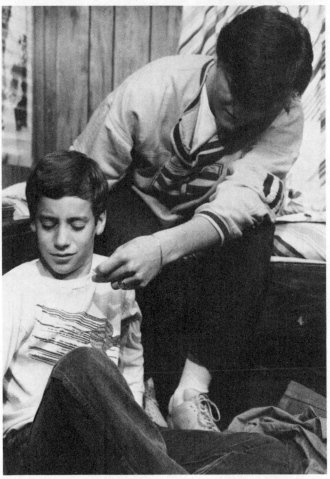

"Try it," Kevin commanded and pushed the lit joint toward Ian's lips. Ian backed away.

"What about you, Billy?" Patrick asked.

"What do you think, Ian?" Billy asked.

"Look at the little big shots," Patrick needled, "having a major meeting about trying a little grass. You're right, Kevin, they're still babies."

A car horn beeped several times outside the open window. "There's my mom," Billy announced, relieved that he had an excuse to get out. "Let's go—we'll be late for soccer."

"Not so fast, squirts. One word to anyone and you'll be sorry. Understand?" Patrick looked down at them.

Ian and Billy shook their heads and ran out of the room.

"Do you think they'll squeal?" Patrick asked Kevin.

"Not Ian. He wouldn't do anything to get me in trouble. I'm in so much hot water now, it almost doesn't make any difference."

Patrick and Kevin spent the rest of the afternoon getting stoned and worrying. This was not a new activity. That's how they spent most afternoons.

"Do you think I should tell my parents?" Ian was still troubled after soccer practice.

"I don't know. I just don't know. That's such a hard decision." Billy felt for his friend.

"Were you going to try it?" Ian asked Billy.

"Not a chance," Billy answered.

"Aren't you even curious?"

"No way. Bev says that stuff really screws up your brain. My sister wouldn't lie to me."

You Should Know

1. What do pot, grass, weed, Mary Jane, joint, roach, and reefer have in common? They are all names that either mean marijuana or relate to the way it is smoked.

2. Marijuana is the dried stems and leaves of the "hemp" plant. When smoked huge numbers of chemicals are released that go sweeping through the body, lungs, and brain.

3. There are some 450 known chemicals in marijuana. When it is smoked these chemicals increase to 2000 or more. The chemicals from a single joint stay in the body for one month.

   The more a person smokes, the more the chemicals build up—eventually with bad effects.

4. The chemical called THC is the one that produces a "high." "Highs" vary. Some say food tastes better, colors seem brighter, music sounds better, they feel more relaxed.

   First-time users and those who smoke too much can panic, become very nervous and very paranoid (think everyone is out to get them).

5. Marijuana smokers have a hard time completing thoughts or concentrating on projects and activities. Regular users become "burnouts." In other words, they are not able to accomplish the things they did before they smoked marijuana.

6. Long-term use of marijuana definitely harms normal body functions. It impairs memory, making it much harder to learn. Marijuana eventually damages brain tissue; can decrease the amount of blood that reaches the heart; causes constant coughs, sore throats, and bronchitis.

7. Marijuana has more cancer-producing elements, tar, and carbon monoxide than cigarettes. Experts say a single joint is equal to a full pack of cigarettes.

Keep in Mind

1. Regular pot users like Kevin become more and more irritable and spend more and more time by themselves.

2. Regular use of marijuana dulls a person's thinking. Kevin's grades dropped steadily because it became more difficult for him to concentrate during class and to remember what he studied when he bothered to study.

3. Young drinkers and pot smokers spend a good deal of their time looking over their shoulders and covering their tracks. They worry constantly about getting caught by parents, teachers, and the police.

4. Heavy users begin to skip meals and feast on junk food, which ultimately affects their health. They sleep for longer and longer periods during the day and neglect personal and family responsibilities.

5. Very often older brothers and sisters "turn on" the younger kids in the family. Many younger children look up to their older siblings and believe that if an older brother or sister smokes pot it must be okay. Wrong. Marijuana has very real physical dangers.

6. Brothers, sisters, parents, and relatives who smoke pot, drink excessively, overeat, or pop pills are not making sound choices for themselves. Although it's often hard to accept, the fact is that people we love and respect sometimes do dangerous and foolish things.

7. It's wise to tell parents about a brother or sister who smokes pot or drinks alcohol. That person may need help and may not get it unless someone speaks out.

Calling All Night

"We have to have a serious talk, Mother. Will you stop paying the bills? Please."

"In a minute," Mrs. Quince answered.

"Please, now?" Niki pleaded.

Mrs. Quince could tell from Niki's tone that she was upset. She closed the checkbook. "What's the matter, Honey?"

"I need your advice. Tomorrow night is Carla's slumber party and I think there's going to be a problem. Well, no, I mean, I think I'm going to have a problem."

"What's that?" her mother asked.

"Sally, Carla's older sister, smokes grass and drinks sometimes."

"She does? What does that have to do with you?" her mother questioned calmly.

"I suppose nothing, but what if Sally gives us a joint or a few cans of beer and everyone is trying it? What should I do? I'm going to feel like a jerk if I don't try it. They may insult me. You know. Or kid me. I am the smallest one. I'm picked on constantly. I'm so small no one asks me to babysit because they think I'm too young. I mean, what I'm asking is will a few puffs on a joint hurt me? Or a couple of sips of beer?"

"No, Niki. They probably won't hurt you."

"What do you think I should do?"

"There are going to be thousands of times in your life that your friends are going to pressure you or you will think they are pushing you to do things you know you should not do or don't want to do. Sometime you will have to learn to stand up to that pressure or you're going to find yourself in situations you don't want to be in. You'll end up doing things that will make you unhappy or leave you feeling guilty.

"Tomorrow night might be a good time for you to tell your friends you don't want to drink, that is if there really is anything to drink. Do you think you can do it?"

"I don't know. I'll try. Thanks for the advice, Mom."

Mrs. Quince knew that keeping Niki home from this slumber party would not prevent her daughter from having to face the same problem a few weeks or a few months later.

"What movie did you get?" Niki asked Carla when they all gathered.

"You'll love it. Sally says it's the best," Carla promised.

"You didn't tell me the name of the movie," Niki's voice had a questioning tone.

"It's called something like *Summer's Nine*."

"I never heard of it."

"Nobody has. It's about a group of teenagers who pack nine weeks of fun into one of those four-week teen-tour vacations. Sally swears it's terrific."

"Sally swore last time," Pam reminded Carla. "That movie was awful."

"It wasn't that bad. My sister can't be right one hundred percent of the time. Give her a break."

"It was horrible," Fran mumbled. "Come on. Let's watch."

"The music's good," Fran commented as they dipped their hands into warm, buttery popcorn.

"It's getting better," Pam announced as they watched a young boy and young girl walk down the beach with their arms around each other. They stopped periodically to kiss and take sips from a can of beer they were sharing.

"I'm liking it. I'm liking it," Niki piped in.

"So you like my choice?" Sally stood in the doorway smiling. Like the couple on the screen, she had a can of beer in her hand, which she held out for them to see. "Want some? It's in the refrigerator. It's mine, not Dad's, so you don't have to worry. There's plenty; I bought extra for everybody."

"Thanks, Sally," Fran said as she jumped up and headed for the kitchen. "Hey, somebody stop the tape."

"Okay." Pam stopped the tape and followed Fran.

"Guess I'll have one, too. What about you, Niki?" Carla asked.

Niki looked lost curled up in the corner of the couch. "I don't think so."

"Why not?"

"I don't know. We really shouldn't be drinking. We're not close to old enough."

"Niki, really. Everybody does it."

Sally, who was still in the doorway, laughed, "Niki, you're the smallest, but the biggest scaredy-cat. It won't hurt you."

"I know that," Niki defended her decision.

Carla shrugged and Fran pointed to Niki. "What's with her?"

"She says we're not old enough," Carla smirked. "Don't have any. See if we care. Somebody put the movie on."

Niki's friends were being mean, but she was going to stick it out and prove to herself and her mother that she could say "No." This wasn't going to be an easy night.

During the film, the girls got up several times for more beer, but Niki was determined to be her own person. Once Pam pointed at the screen and said to Niki, "See what you're going to miss. They're drinking, and look at the great time they're having."

"You know, Niki," Fran explained her point of view, "sooner or later you're going to have to join in. My brother and I drink whenever our parents are out. Vince says I'm better off drinking with him than some crazy little boys my own age. 'They'll get you sick or take advantage of you,' he said."

"I'm not sure I ever want to drink." Niki attempted to be honest with her friends and tell them how she felt. They snickered. If she couldn't talk to Carla, Fran, and Pam, well, she thought, she couldn't talk about this to anyone. These were her best friends in the world.

"How do you know you don't want to drink until you try it?" Fran pressed on.

"I don't want to; I don't feel right about it. My mother doesn't think I should be drinking yet and I kind of agree with her."

"You mean she talks to you about drinking?" Carla was horrified.

Niki nodded yes. "That's how I decided I wasn't going to drink. I thought I was, but when we got into it, I changed my mind."

"What did your mother say?" Carla was curious.

"She didn't say much. Mostly that drinking was my choice."

"Pam, did your mother talk to you?" Fran asked, but Pam didn't answer.

"Pam!" Fran shouted.

"She fell asleep," Niki offered, happy that they had turned the discussion away from her.

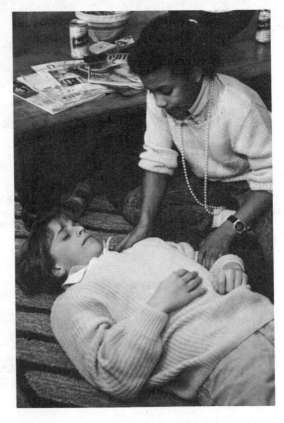

"How could she? It's only nine-thirty." Fran didn't believe Pam was sleeping. She shook her, but there was no reaction. "Hey, come here. Pam's breathing funny. Like she can't get air. She's not asleep. What's wrong?" Fran looked at her friends for an answer.

"Come on, Pam, that's enough," Fran urged, "the joke is over. You can't be that bombed on a couple of beers."

The girls looked at one another; there was no sound in the room except for Pam's strange nonbreathing. She sounded like a wounded animal.

"Niki, go get my sister. She's in her room. How much did she have to drink?" Carla asked the others. No one knew.

Sally raced into the room. "What's the matter?"

"Listen to Pam. I never heard anything like that. Have you?" Fran thought maybe Sally, who was older, might know what was wrong.

"How much did she drink?" Sally asked.

"No one knows," Carla answered her sister.

"Somebody look in the refrigerator." Sally was panicked. She had seen lots of kids drunk and passed out, but this was different. Pam was scary. The breathing sound was getting harder to hear; the breaths were becoming shorter. "We have to do something quickly. Call Emergency at the hospital. Fran, you do that. Ask them what's the fastest way to get someone there. Explain exactly how Pam is acting. Carla, go in my room and use my phone to call Pam's parents. I hope they're home."

"Me?" Carla was terrified. "What will I say?"

"Carla, this is no time to be a baby. Tell them to meet us in Saint Joseph's Emergency Room. Just say that Pam is unconscious and I took her there because we were worried about her. Don't say anything else. Understand? I'll take the blame for the beer when we get her to the hospital."

Fran came back. "They're sending the First Aid Squad."

"Niki, find a blanket. Pam is shaking." Sally knelt next to Pam searching for a sign that she was coming around. The girls hovered. All silent. All terrified.

"I did it," Carla told her sister. "They're on their way. Pam's mother said something strange. She said, 'I hope Pam took her pills.' Then she sounded real upset. 'Oh, no. Pam couldn't have forgotten them. She knows she can't do that.' What pills? I didn't know Pam took pills or was sick."

"Oh, no," was all Sally got to say before the doorbell rang.

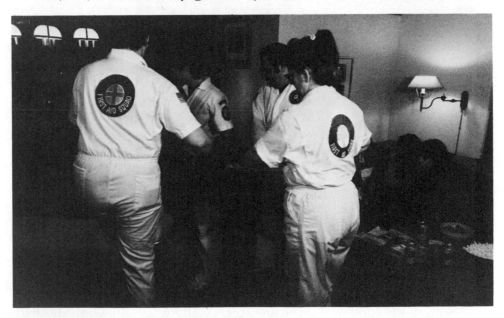

The emergency crew strapped Pam to a stretcher—fast. Everyone stayed back out of their way. "Where are her parents?" one of the men asked.

"On their way to the hospital," Sally answered.

"One of you come with us." He looked at Sally.

"Carla, find Mother. I think she and Daddy are at the Smiths' planning Mr. Smith's campaign. Try there first. Then try the Grahams' or the McFarleys'. Tell them to meet us at the hospital."

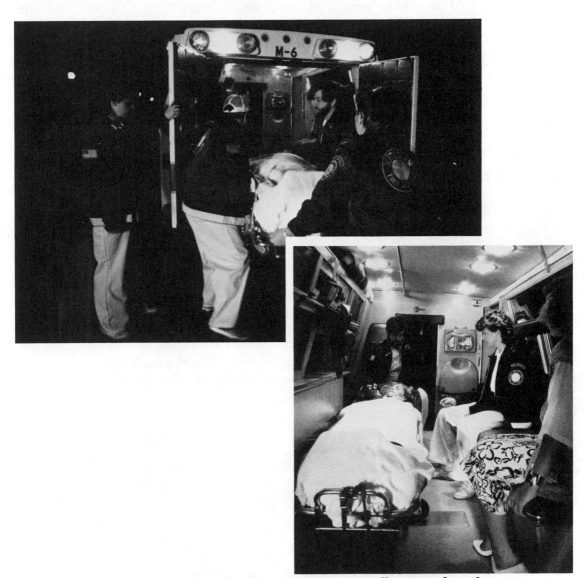

In the ambulance, Pam was given oxygen. Sally stared at her horrified at what she had done to her little sister's friend. She didn't know exactly what was wrong with Pam, but she knew it was serious. As the ambulance raced through the streets with its siren blaring, Sally became more fearful of facing Pam's parents.

Mr. and Mrs. O'Leary were pacing and looking out the window for the ambulance. They followed the stretcher. Sally was alone in the waiting room. She wrapped her arms around each other and repeated to herself, "Pam will be okay; Pam will be okay."

After what seemed like a year to Sally, Mrs. O'Leary and the doctor came out. Mrs. O'Leary looked at her pleadingly, "You must tell us the truth. Did Pam drink any alcohol?"

"Yes," Sally said weakly, her stomach dropping.

"That's what I thought," the doctor commented.

"She didn't have much. One, maybe two beers. The girls weren't sure."

"It's not your fault, Sally." Mrs. O'Leary sunk into one of the waiting room chairs. "It's mine. Pam has epilepsy, but she's on medication that controls it. She's not permitted any alcohol, but I never told her. I figured having epilepsy was enough. It never entered my mind that she would drink. She's so young."

"But I'm the one who gave them the beer."

Mrs. O'Leary was too upset to talk. "Why don't you go home. We'll call you later."

"No. I'm staying."

•   •   •

"Don't leave me," Carla begged her friends. "My mother will be furious. I'm scared. Don't call your mothers yet."

"Maybe it would be better if my mother or Fran's were here," Niki suggested. She called her mom.

Mrs. Quince stayed with the girls until Carla's parents returned from the hospital. No one said much. Everyone was thinking about Pam.

Sally and her parents arrived home about one o'clock in the morning. They reported that Pam was doing better but they wouldn't know anything more until the morning. Carla's mother explained epilepsy and Pam's reaction to alcohol.

"I didn't know there was anything wrong with Pam," Fran said.

"Why didn't she tell us?" Niki shook her head as she and her mother left for home.

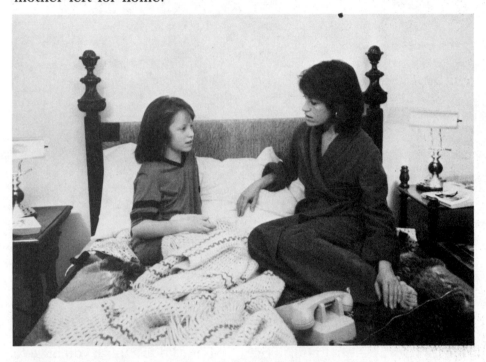

"What if she dies?" Niki asked her mother.

"Don't even think that. Go to bed."

"That's what we're all thinking, isn't it?"

"I suppose," her mother agreed.

"Call the hospital, please."

"Niki, we've been calling all night," Mrs. Quince reminded her daughter.

"I know, but maybe this time the report will be better."

"Okay." Mrs. Quince was hopeful. Once again she dialed Saint Joseph's and asked for the condition of Pamela O'Leary. She waited while her call was transferred to the Intensive Care Unit.

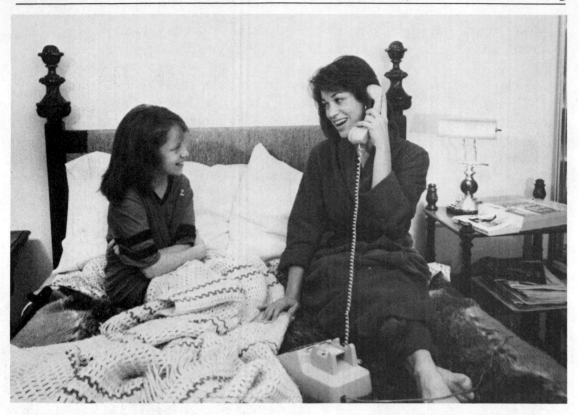

"She's off the critical list," the nurse reported this time. "As of twenty minutes ago. You probably already know that since you and the others have been calling every hour."

"Thank you," Mrs. Quince told the nurse. "We won't call again tonight."

Mrs. Quince smiled as she told Niki the good news. Niki cried. Her friend was going to be all right. "Mom, I don't think you have to worry about me drinking."

You Should Know

1. Mixing drugs of any kind—remember, alcohol *is* a drug—can kill you. Don't do it. Ever. For any reason.

2. Drinking when taking any prescription drug is extraordinarily dangerous. Look at this tranquilizer example: The combination of a drink and tranquilizer hits the body *eight* times more powerfully than either of those two drugs would by itself.

3. This reaction explains why Pam, who was taking medication to control her epilepsy, became violently ill.

4. Alcohol acts faster on girls than on boys. A male has more water and less fat in his body (alcohol does not dissolve in fat). The additional water helps weaken the strength of the alcohol as it enters the bloodstream.

   When the same size boy and girl drink the same amount, the girl will have a higher level of alcohol in her blood.

5. Right before the menstrual period, the body absorbs alcohol faster than other times. At these times, the amount of alcohol in the blood will shoot up even faster.

6. Alcohol is loaded with calories. Anyone who drinks fairly regularly can count on watching the numbers on a scale go higher. Most drinks contain between 100 and 150 calories. One beer has about 125 calories.

   "Light" beers are no diet bargain either—maybe 25 fewer calories than a regular beer with about the same amount of alcohol. So you probably won't be any more sober or thinner if you drink "lite" beers.

7. Boy or girl, alcohol can be murder on the face. It stimulates fat and oil production. Like greasy french fries, chocolate, and potato chips, alcohol can make skin problems worse.

Keep in Mind

1. Not all kids are lucky enough to have an understanding parent like Niki's mother. Many parents would go crazy if they heard or thought that alcohol or pot was going to be available anywhere their children were going to be. It is much easier to say "No" when a parent understands your dilemma.

2. If a parent is as trusting as Niki's mother, it seems silly to ruin such a good relationship over drinking. All choices—and there will be thousands of them—will be easier and more of them will go your way with a parent on your side.

3. Talk to friends about drinking. Make your position clear. Don't be a fence-sitter. Niki sounded weak and unsure: "I don't think so," she said when asked if she wanted a beer. She should have said what she meant; she should have said "No."

4. A strong person can't be shamed into drinking. She simply says, "It's not what I want to do." Friends will leave her alone if she takes a firm position without judging them, without saying things like, "You shouldn't be drinking."

5. Sometimes being that straightforward is too difficult. Other reasons can be as effective, but easier for some people:

   · "Drinking makes me sick."

   · "Not tonight. I don't feel very well."

   · "Can't handle it."

   · "I've tried it. There's not much to it."

   · "Can't stand the taste otherwise I'd drink."

6. Any horrible drinking experience such as vomiting on someone's rug (ugh!) or on the sweater you borrowed from your older sister, or passing out in front of your friends will stick with you for years. What these girls lived through, the very serious reaction to mixing drugs, is the kind of experience that stays in mind forever. Whenever any of them drinks, she will undoubtedly think of Pam.

Chapter 8

Robinson, Ryan, Sorvetta

Not much had gone wrong during Jamie's first week at his new school. He had heard that the high school was really rough, that the kids pushing dope cornered you in bathrooms, blocked you in the schoolyard, and made life in general pretty tough if you didn't buy what they were selling and tougher if you couldn't pay up.

Jamie was scared. He stuck close to his friend Pete whenever they were in the schoolyard or walking home from school. Jamie believed there was safety in numbers. He was hardly a sissy, but Jamie knew that when it came to drugs, the drinkers and druggers were different. Those guys had hard-core toughness. They stopped at nothing to get what they wanted.

Last year Jamie had seen Cal Ryan and his buddies knocking some poor kid's head against the side of the building. He and his dad were driving by, but Jamie did not point it out. No sense in upsetting him, Jamie had thought. He knew his parents were worried about his going to the high school. Showing his father that scene only would have alarmed them further.

Jamie thought he could take care of himself. He didn't consider himself a coward, but something inside him kept saying it's just plain smart to stay away from Cal.

The first day of math class Jamie spotted Cal and selected a seat on the other side of the classroom, but within a few days the teacher decided they would sit in alphabetical order until he could learn their names. "Jamie Robinson, there, Cal Ryan, next to Robinson, Sorvetta, you start this new row behind Ryan, right here."

"So, there I was," Jamie explained to Pete, "not only am I next to Ryan, but he's already told me he is going to look at my paper during all tests. Can you believe it? He doesn't ask me if he can cheat from my paper, he tells me."

"What are you going to do?" Pete asked.

"I'm going to hope this math guy can learn our names before the first test."

"And if he doesn't?" Pete persisted.

"I'd like to be sick that day and take a makeup by myself."

"Good, genius, but that's not going to work."

"I know. I'll think of something," Jamie assured Pete as much as himself.

"What's Ryan doing in your math class?" Pete asked

"This is the third time he's taken that class," Jamie told him. "Guess he plans on staying in high school forever."

"He's getting a little old. Don't you think he's embarrassed sitting with a bunch of freshmen. Does he know you're only in eighth grade?" Pete asked.

"I'm not going to tell him. Now I wished they hadn't moved me ahead. I thought it was a great honor to be taking freshman math this year. I'm not so sure."

When he was in class, which wasn't very often, Cal Ryan ignored Jamie. He took his seat and stared off into space. Mr. Wilkey knew better than to call on Cal or request his homework.

Much to Jamie's surprise, Cal showed up for the first test. He winked at Jamie, and Jamie recognized that he had to stand up to Ryan that minute or let him copy from his paper. Cheating seemed less threatening than having Cal and his friends breathing down his neck. Mr. Wilkey collected the papers and dismissed the class. Jamie was depressed.

On the way home Jamie and Pete agreed that this was a bad way to begin five years in a new school. They decided Jamie should talk over the problem with his parents.

• • •

"It doesn't bother those guys to work you over. I've seen them do it," Jamie explained to his mother.

Instead of hitting the ceiling, she was sympathetic. She admitted that Jamie was in a bind and understood why he was afraid of Cal Ryan. His mother was worried, but she wanted Jamie to fight his own battles. "I think you have to speak to Mr. Wilkey."

"What will I say? 'Mr. Wilkey, Cal cheated on the equations test.' I'll sound like a tattletale."

"If Cal's repeating for the third time, Mr. Wilkey has already figured out he didn't get a passing grade by himself. You won't have too much explaining to do," his mother said.

The following day Cal walked into math class and handed Jamie an envelope. "Thanks for yesterday. Put it away before Wilkey gets here."

Jamie felt the lumpy envelope. It could only be a couple of joints. "Here." Jamie passed the envelope back. "I don't want any, thanks. Keep it."

"Listen, kid, most people pay, but you're doing me a big favor. I have to pass this class."

"Really, it's okay," Jamie insisted when Cal forced the envelope back into his hand.

"Sit down, everyone. Let's begin. Ryan, quiet." Mr. Wilkey had appeared in the front of the classroom.

Cal sat silently next to a nervous Jamie Robinson, who slipped the envelope into his notebook. Some gift, he thought. Dope.

The instant the bell rang Cal was out the door. Jamie approached Mr. Wilkey. "When can I see you, Mr. Wilkey?" he asked.

"What's the problem, Jamie? You are Jamie, aren't you?"

"Yes."

"You're one of the eighth graders, but it's certainly not the work. I graded your paper last night."

"It's about the test." Mr. Wilkey listened. "And Cal Ryan," Jamie forced out the name.

"You stay away from him, Jamie."

"That's just it. I'm trying, but you put him next to me and I let him copy my test paper. I sort of had no choice."

"You did!" Mr. Wilkey raised his eyebrows. "I never would have known. That guy can't even copy correctly."

"Can you move my seat without Cal knowing that I spoke to you?"

"Sure. I'll pretend I've learned everyone's name and tomorrow I'll announce that beginning Monday students may sit wherever they like. Jamie, Ryan's trouble. Stay away," Mr. Wilkey advised kindly.

"Thank you." Jamie left the room clutching his notebook so that the envelope would not drop onto the floor.

"He didn't fail me or say a word about the cheating," Jamie told Pete.

"Of course not," Pete educated his friend. "The teachers know what's going on."

They were discussing whether to try the pot or give it back when they walked into Cal and Eddie sitting on the back steps. "Showing off your stash?" Cal asked. "Want some of your own, Pete?"

"Can I think about it? I don't have money with me," Pete answered nervously.

"Yeah, yeah, sure. You think about it. Let me know. Okay?" Cal started to walk away.

"Wait. Take this back," Jamie tried again to return the marijuana.

"Nope. You were good to me, so I was good to you. We'll keep it that way, right?" Cal smiled broadly.

Jamie nodded but he felt threatened.

The following day in math class Mr. Wilkey made his seating announcement and returned the tests. Cal glared at Jamie, "What did you get?"

Jamie tilted his paper to show his 90. He could see Cal's fat, red 52. At that moment Jamie hated math class; he hated the high school. He didn't want to be smart anymore; it wasn't fun being pushed ahead. Jamie wanted to go back to his old school.

The test didn't stop Cal. For weeks he trapped Pete and Jamie outside school. He caught up with them in the cafeteria or in the bathroom. The question was the same: "You guys ready?"

They gave the same answer: "No, we're not interested." In a way, having Cal and Eddie greet them in the hall made Jamie and Pete feel grown-up and part of the high school.

Then suddenly, Cal stopped bugging them. He didn't look at Jamie in math class. Cal and his buddies stopped teasing them and following them. They ignored Jamie and his friends totally.

"Guess they gave up on us," Pete said, laughing. "They got the message that we're not buying. They must have found some other suckers."

You Should Know

1. It is very easy to develop a psychological dependence on marijuana. A person thinks he needs and must have this drug to get through the day. This type of craving is often as strong as physical dependence in which the body actually reacts if the drug is missing.

2. As with alcohol, tolerance to pot builds up. It takes more and more marijuana to get high.

3. The signs of drug use quickly become obvious to teachers and school officials. Mr. Wilkey had long been aware of Cal's marijuana problem because Cal showed many of the signs of someone who is dependent on a drug. For the past two years, Cal had been cutting classes, turning in fewer and fewer assignments, and coming to school looking sloppy.

4. In many schools teachers, principals, and other staff must, by state, city, or school rule, report drug offenders to authorities. In some instances, school officials have the right to search lockers and/or the students themselves.

5. Students who are abusing alcohol, pot, or other drugs are referred to Student Assistance Programs, which are available in many states. A student who is recognized as having a drug problem or any student who feels he may be developing one is evaluated by a professional, then sent for counseling and necessary treatment.

6. In an effort to have students ask for help *before* their drug problems are out of control, most Student Assistance Programs keep participation confidential.

7. Supporting a pot "habit" requires increasingly larger amounts of money. After borrowing the limit from parents, brothers, and sisters, the user dips into his savings account. Grandparents get "hit" for a loan. When easy sources are depleted, the user begins to sell off his possessions and steal. Eventually, to keep himself supplied he becomes a dealer.

Keep in Mind

1. You don't have to have a drinking, marijuana, or other drug problem to use the drug counseling services in your school. If a druggie is bothering you, your friends are pressuring you, or you simply have a question, make an appointment.

Perhaps your parents can't or won't talk to you or you are afraid to talk to them about drugs. Under such circumstances it is wise to consult a school counselor. Many are trained to help.

2. Very often, a "tough-guy" act such as Cal's is a cover for real problems. Anyone who thinks he's too dumb, too fat, too thin, lousy at basketball, terrible at dancing, or the worst in math should take serious steps to change his thinking or to correct the problem.

What a person believes about himself (his "self-image") is probably not a hundred percent correct, but if that's the way he feels, working on what's wrong should help. A diet, extra help in math, or practice from the foul line will do more to change someone's self-image than burying unhappiness in cans of beer or ounces of marijuana.

3. Research has shown that young people who abuse alcohol, pot, and other drugs do not grow up. They remain immature because they hide their feelings behind drugs. Once sober or straight, the same person with the same problems is waiting.

4. The outgoing achiever who becomes involved with marijuana begins to slip on all fronts: at home, at school, with friends, in sports. He replaces his high achievement and goal-oriented attitude with an "I don't care" one. He begins to believe he doesn't care, but he does.

Chapter 9

A Good Lie

"**M**om, hurry up. I'm going to the dance, not you. You can finish dressing for your company when you get back. Maggie's waiting," Cynthia urged.

"I'm coming. Call Maggie and tell her we'll be there in five minutes," Mrs. Collins shouted as she came downstairs. "Hey, you look adorable."

"Thanks, Mom, but don't you think I'm getting a bit old to look 'adorable'? Baby Kyle is adorable."

"You'll always be adorable to me." Her mother brushed back Cynthia's hair and kissed her forehead.

Cindy rearranged her bangs and called Maggie. "We're on our way—finally. Yes, I have my things in my hand."

As they pulled up in front of the school gym, they could hear the music. "I wonder if Warren is going to dance with fat Marsha." When Maggie said this, both girls broke up giggling.

"Really, girls. Sometimes you are so unkind," Mrs. Collins reprimanded them.

"Mom, she is very fat."

"Go. I don't want to get into it. Have a good time. Maggie, your sister Ingrid will be here to pick you up at ten?"

"Yes, Mrs. Collins, don't worry. She'll be here."

"Mom, don't forget to drop my bag at Maggie's."

"I won't. Have fun, you two, and don't stay up all night talking."

"Hi, Cindy, want to dance?"

Cindy couldn't believe her luck. Jonathan Newcomb walked up to her and asked her to dance. A dream come true.

"Sure, Jon," Cindy replied.

"Pretty good dance. More people than the last one. Don't you think?"

"Definitely," Cindy answered. "By the way, how's history? Mrs. Bailey is so boring. I miss not having you in my class like last year." Cindy hoped she hadn't admitted too much.

"It's different. Our class is very small. You have to do the home-work or you're dead. Know what I mean? Last year there was always someone like you who had the answers."

Cindy figured that was Jonathan's way of saying that he missed her, too. She repeated the conversation to Maggie while they waited for Ingrid. Finally Ingrid drove up. Most of the others had gone home.

Maggie opened the front door and Cindy heard her groan at her sister. "Oh, Ingrid, not again."

Ingrid yelled, "Look, kid, I'm doing you a favor. Get in."

Cindy thought Ingrid sounded funny. "Get in" came out as one word, but Cindy wasn't sure. She whispered to Maggie, "What do you mean by 'not again'?"

Maggie was embarrassed. "My sister's been drinking."

Ingrid got out of the car and began talking very loudly, "Cindy, get your butt in the car. You, too, Mags."

Cindy was pretty sure Ingrid was drunk. Ingrid was usually very quiet and didn't give orders or use words like "butt."

"Maggie, go ahead. I'll get another ride."

"But how?" Maggie objected. "Almost everyone has gone. Don't be silly. Ingrid can drive. She got here, didn't she?" Maggie defended her sister.

"I know that, but I don't think it's a good idea. Send your sister home or wherever she's going and wait with me. I'll call my mother or my uncle."

"But your parents have company. Mine would have a fit if I interrupted their party."

Cindy wasn't sure if her parents would mind. She made another suggestion. "We'll ask one of the teachers."

"That will get Ingrid in all kinds of trouble. Besides, if she goes home without us—" Maggie continued, not keeping her thoughts together. "It's only a short ride to my house. Your stuff is there. You're spending the night. Come on, Cindy, please."

"Are you girls getting in or not?" Ingrid shouted. "I haven't got all night. They're waiting for me at Pauline's. I'd like to get back to the party."

"That's just what you need," Maggie muttered under her breath.

The louder Ingrid was, the more frightened Cindy became. "Maggie, I'm not getting in the car. Your sister is drunk. I'll find a way home, if I have to walk."

"You can't do that. You have to come." Maggie pulled on Cindy's sleeve.

"I won't go. If you won't wait for my mother, go on. That's final," she whispered.

"Okay, okay," Maggie slammed the front door. "Let's go, Ingrid."

"What about Cindy?"

"She's not coming. Her mother is picking her up."

"How come?"

"Because you're drunk, Ingrid."

"I had a few drinks. So what? I can still drive perfectly well."

Cindy wanted them to leave. She was getting more and more upset and unsure of her decision. Ingrid repeated that she could drive. Maybe she could. Maybe I'm just being silly, Cindy told herself. It was too far to walk home. If she asked a teacher for a ride, well, that would call for a "public" explanation. That was too terrible to think about. What were Ingrid's parents going to say when Cindy didn't spend the night? The easiest thing to do would be to get in the car.

"I can drive, Cindy. Honest." Cindy did not believe Ingrid.

Cindy's voice shook. This was the first time she had to deal with someone who was drunk. "Thanks, Ingrid. I don't feel very well. I want to sleep home tonight. My mother or father will come for me."

Ingrid bought the lie. Cindy turned and went to call her house. "Oh, Dad, you're there." Just hearing her father's voice made her cry.

"Cindy, what's the matter? Of course, I'm here. You knew we were home. Are you hurt? Where are you?" Mr. Collins was alarmed.

Cindy couldn't talk. "Cindy, answer me."

"I'm okay. Come get me."

"Where's Maggie's sister? Where are you?"

"School. I'm at school."

"What happened?" Mr. Collins asked.

"Dad, please. I'll tell you later."

"Don't move. I'll be right there."

The assistant principal saw Cindy talking on the pay phone and walked in her direction. She dried her eyes. "Are you all right, Cynthia?" he asked.

"Yes, thank you."

"Do you need a ride?"

"My father is on his way. Thanks, anyway."

While she waited she tried to figure out what she was going to tell her father. She could say she didn't feel well. No, she couldn't lie to her father. Cindy recalled the television commercial she and her mother had watched: Four teenagers were in a car, laughing and drinking and passing a bottle of liquor. Suddenly there was a loud crash. Sitting in the same seats were four spooky skeletons. Two

were crushed up. Although it was warm, Cindy shivered. She hoped
Maggie and Ingrid got home safely.

"I didn't ruin your party, did I?" Cindy asked her father.

"No, Honey. You know you're the most important thing in the
world to us. What happened?"

"I did the right thing, I think. Ingrid was drunk. Well, maybe not
drunk, but she had had some drinks at a party. She was talking
funny. I was afraid to get in the car."

Mr. Collins hugged his daughter to reassure her. "If you need
help or a ride, no matter where we are or what we're doing, your
mother or I will get you or find someone to bring you home safely."

103

You Should Know

1. Auto accidents kill fourteen teenagers every day.

2. Many of these victims are teenagers who made the mistake of riding with someone who had been drinking. In fact, the number of teenage *passengers* who die almost equals the number of teenage *drivers* who lose their lives.

3. Usually people who have difficulty talking, whose speech is slurred or jumbled as Ingrid's was, have a blood alcohol level of .10 percent. In most states a person with this level is considered legally intoxicated. A person driving with that much alcohol in her blood is *twelve times* more likely to have an accident than someone who is sober.

4. If it still sounds as if adults are making too big a deal about drinking and driving, consider this: All states have laws concerning how often a person can be picked up legally intoxicated before drastic action is taken.
    In New York, for example, two offenses of .10 or more in *ten years* can lead to four years in prison! Driving and drinking is *that* serious.

5. No matter what the driver says, alcohol reduces his or her ability to drive safely. A person only *thinks* her reactions and judgment are sharp. The more alcohol, the less skillful the driver will be.

6. "It's only a short ride" is a poor excuse. Most accidents happen close to home.

7. Coffee, cold showers, and fresh air do not sober up a person. Only time does.

Keep in Mind

1. No matter how far you have to go, no one is doing you a favor if she offers you a ride after she has been drinking.

2. Don't get in a car driven by *anyone* who has been drinking. Everyone has only one life. Taking that kind of chance with it is plain stupid.

3. What Cindy had to do (refuse to get in the car with Maggie's sister) is a hundred times harder if the driver is a parent, say, a best friend's father. No matter how old you are, you can tell that parent to wait, you have to call your mother to tell her something, anything. Make up something. Any lie that keeps you out of a drunk driver's car is a good one.

Then get on the phone and tell your mother or father that Mr. Whoever seems drunk to you. Your parent will tell you not to get in the car; go back and tell him your mother said you are to wait for her. Go on without me.

4. Now is the time to discuss rides home from movies, dances, classes, games, and other special activities. Explain to your parents that you want emergency people to call so that you never feel you must ride with a person who has been drinking. Memorize or keep their telephone numbers with you. A list might include an aunt or an uncle, one or two neighbors, a friend's parents, and the nearest taxicab company if there is one in the area.

If a parent says, "Don't worry, no one is going to be drunk when they pick you up," be firm. Ask that parent how she can be so sure. No one has control over what other people do. Tell your parent you will feel better if you have "safe rides" you can call if you need one.

5. Cindy handled Ingrid very well. It's often useless to argue with someone who has been drinking. It's best to stay calm and explain what you plan to do.

6. Keeping Ingrid's or anyone else's drinking a secret is not helping or protecting them. Young people who drink must realize they are taking risks and can cause serious harm to themselves and others, especially if they are driving cars.

7. It's always a good idea, if parents are out, to know how to reach them.

8. Most parents feel as Mr. Collins did: His child's safety is more important than anything he could possibly be doing. Ask your parents. Chances are they will tell you the same thing.

Chapter 10

Battle of the Bands

Megan had waited months for Dennis to ask her out. Her friend Kristen heard from one of the older boys that Dennis planned to, but he sure had been slow about it. One Monday he hurried past her at dismissal. "Want to go to the Battle of the Bands Saturday afternoon?" he asked.

"Sure." Megan smiled, too surprised to think of anything else.

"I'll pick you up at one," he added and was down the street and out of sight before Megan finished saying "fine."

Megan couldn't help but think on her way home how jealous Sybil and Kristen were going to be. Dennis was considered about the best catch in the whole school. Everyone would be at the band concert. It was a statewide, school-sponsored contest. Everyone would see her with Dennis.

She, Kristen, and Sybil consulted on what she would wear. Megan tried on everything she owned, plus everything from Kristen's and Sybil's wardrobes that fit her. After Megan modeled many outfits, they finally agreed on her new swirly print dress and Kristen's white jacket. As it turned out Megan felt it would not have made one bit of difference if she had worn the jeans and sweatshirt she reserved for cleaning the garage.

Dennis rang the bell at one o'clock sharp. He looked great, cuter than he did in school, Megan thought. He looked older, too, but then he was an upperclassman. This was her first date with one of the older guys, and she was nervous.

"Hi," Megan said shyly. "Want to come in for a minute?"

Dennis shook his head. "We better go so we can get good seats."

"Okay. Bye, Mom, see you later," Megan called to her mother.

"What's the hurry? You have plenty of time. Have Dennis come in for a minute."

"Can't. We want to get good seats."

Megan and Dennis walked along in silence at first. Megan realized she would have to start the conversation. "What do you think of the new principal? She's pretty strange, isn't she?"

"Yeah."

"I thought we'd get someone older, didn't you?"

"I suppose." Dennis seemed not to know or care that Megan was walking with him.

To whatever Megan said, Dennis grunted or answered sharply. She decided he didn't like her. He stopped suddenly and looked around strangely to see if anyone was in sight. He slipped into the driveway behind the theater.

"What's wrong?" Megan asked.

"Nothing."

"What are you doing?" Megan watched. "What's in that bottle?"

Dennis had tipped a small bottle up to his mouth and was drinking something.

"It's vodka. Want some?"

"No. Of course not. Are you nuts? You going to keep that stuff with you inside?"

"Sure."

"But if you get caught, you'll be thrown out of school. This is like a basketball game or a dance. It's a school event."

"I know," Dennis answered, but he didn't seem to care. He screwed the top back on the bottle and started walking.

Megan felt funny, as if *she* were doing something wrong.

The local theater where the concert was being held was pretty crowded by the time they arrived, but they found two seats near some of Dennis's friends who also had dates. Megan was friendly to Ladd, Paul, and Trevor, but more quiet than usual. She watched Dennis's jacket which he held tightly under his arm. Kristen and Sybil had to scream to get her attention even though they were only two rows behind her. She waved weakly at them and did not look back when Dennis and his friends left their seats.

"Something's wrong," Sybil told Kristen. "Meg doesn't look happy. She waited and waited for a date with Dennis. Something's wrong. I'm telling you."

After the concert, kids stampeded out. "Wait here," Dennis told Megan. He went back to the men's room, she guessed.

When Kristen and Sybil leaned across the two rows of seats and tapped her on the shoulder, Megan jumped. "Having fun?" they asked.

"Sure." Megan faked a smile to get rid of them.

"Talk to you later," Sybil called as she was shoved into the aisle.

Dennis and Megan were the last to leave. This gave Megan an odd feeling. As soon as they were away from the theater, Dennis pulled her between two buildings and took out his bottle.

"Want some now?" he asked.

Megan hesitated, thinking _he will think I'm a terrible sissy. He'll never ask me out again._ "Later," she said, pushing off her decision and giving her more time to think about what to do.

Her mother had talked to her about dates and boys making sexual advances. Although she had not had to use her knowledge yet, she knew what to do. But her mother had not talked to her about drinking. She had no idea of what to do. She knew Sybil and Kristen were given wine at family parties, weddings, and religious celebrations. She had had champagne at her aunt's wedding but didn't like it. There was something about the idea of drinking on the street out of a bottle with a boy that made Megan feel guilty just thinking about it.

Dennis swallowed with a big gulping sound, and they started to walk. "How about a pizza?"

"Sounds good," Megan agreed. Anything to get where there were people so that Dennis could not ask her if she wanted a drink. She was worried nonetheless. "You're not going to drink in there?"

"You must really think I'm stupid."

Inside Dennis became very talkative, and Megan started to relax. He discussed the concert and his friend Ladd's new dog. He talked about his father's new car and his sister's boyfriend, whom he hated.

For the first time all afternoon, Megan was happy to be out with Dennis. He was funny. He made crazy faces and mimicked some of the teachers. He did a great Mr. Adler, one of the guidance counselors and the most hysterical imitation of Mrs. Summer, the principal, talking fast and throwing his arms around the way she did when she was angry at one of the students. Megan laughed so hard she could barely get her pizza down.

The minute they were back outside Dennis ducked out of sight. Megan felt foolish standing as if she were his bodyguard, ready to warn him that his enemies were approaching.

"Let's go home," Megan said.

"In a minute. Why don't you have some? You'll feel better." This time when Dennis asked, there was a threatening sound in his voice. Megan felt the way she did when her parents asked her to do something she didn't think was fair. She was angry, but at the same time she was fearful of what would happen if she refused.

"Ladd's date is drinking. So are Paul's, and Trevor's."

"How do you know that?" Megan asked, not really caring about the answer.

"Ladd told me when we were drinking in the bathroom at the concert."

"Oh." Megan didn't know what to do.

"You'll understand someday," Dennis told her and sat down.

She hated his acting like that, as if she were a child. She knew that if she didn't drink, if she didn't become "one of the boys," as Ladd's, Paul's, and Trevor's dates were doing, Dennis wasn't going to ask her out again.

Whatever Dennis said made her feel worse. "It's only vodka. No one will know. You can't smell it or anything. Aren't you going to feel dumb when you're the only girl who doesn't drink on dates? You know who will be really pleased?"

"Who?" Megan started up the steps.

"Your mother, that's who." Dennis laughed.

"Very funny," Megan said, but she didn't think it was funny at all. She was hating Dennis and thinking should she have a sip just to shut him up. She couldn't stand it.

"This is your last chance

to act like a grown-up before you go back to your mommy. What do you say?"

"Leave me alone," Megan yelled, "I'll see you." She left Dennis on the steps.

The bum, she said to herself as she walked home. She liked Dennis. She had wanted to please him. At the Pizza House she really thought he was having a good time. She was, but she wasn't going to drink because Paul's and Trevor's dates were drinking. She wasn't about to let any guy tell her what to do.

Dennis called the next day. "Man, was I sick. Were you okay?" he asked Megan.

"I'm fine," Megan responded, at first confused by his question.

"Want to go to the dance next Saturday?" Dennis asked as if he had been a perfect date.

"I don't know." Megan realized that Dennis did not remember how offensive he had been.

"I won't drink. Nothing." He groaned to indicate how sick he was. "My head still hurts and it's one o'clock in the afternoon."

"I'll ask my mother and tell you in school on Monday. Okay?" Megan wanted to think this one over.

You Should Know

1. Many people fear that another person or group will not like them if they don't do what is wanted or expected of them. Megan was afraid that Dennis would not like her because she refused to drink. To like someone because she or he drinks is a very shallow reason. Friendships built on drinking don't usually last, and if they do they are rarely happy or fun.

2. Alcohol makes it more difficult to resist sexual advances or to say "No" to more alcohol or to other drugs. Similarly, alcohol makes it harder to refuse challenges and dares. "Under the influence" many people do things they would not otherwise do.

3. Everyone has a built-in alarm system that warns against physical danger: We walk cautiously on ice, stay back from the edges of high places, keep our hands out of fire. A warning signal races to the brain when someone asks us to do something we're not sure we want to do. Listen to the warning feeling whenever you have it.

4. Very frequently drinkers don't remember how they act. If Dennis had any recall of his behavior he would not have had the nerve to call Megan for another date.

Keep in Mind

1. Megan could have abandoned Dennis on the way to the concert. His drinking was making her nervous. Had she returned home she would not have had to worry during the concert that the bottle was going to be discovered.

2. Megan did not have to feel guilty about Dennis's drinking. She is only responsible for herself and her own actions.

3. Many boys and men think it is masculine to drink. They believe that drinking makes them more appealing to the opposite sex. It is neither macho nor sexy when males drink. Dennis was, from Megan's point of view, being pushy and obnoxious.

4. Likewise, females wrongly think they will be more sought after if they do what they are told or if they drink when alcohol is offered.

5. Do not hesitate to use promises or parents' rules to get out of a situation. Megan could have left Dennis at any point by saying, "I forgot, I have to babysit at three" or "I said I'd be home right after the concert." Not exactly the truth, but it would have done the trick.

6. Megan's strength and the ability to say "No" and walk away are in all of us. We need to use it more often.

Chapter 11

Oh, Brother

"Don't you have band practice on Thursday nights?" Kelly asked her younger brother as they cleaned up the kitchen after dinner.

"Not tonight." Mike looked down when he answered. He couldn't tell his sister the truth on her first night home from college. He would tell her about band, photography club, and his grades after his grandparents' anniversary party. She was going to be furious . . . and disappointed.

Kelly had been so proud of Mike when he won first prize in a national photography contest last year. His complex double exposure of football players tackling each other in the middle of a swimming pool had been shipped to New York City for a monthlong showing in a famous art gallery. His mother had said, "That's wonderful. Go tell your father. We'll celebrate."

Mike's mother and father started with a bottle of champagne. Mike had a few sips; Kelly refused. Mr. and Mrs. Greer's celebration went on long into the night. That was the last time either of them mentioned the honor, but Kelly carried on for weeks. "Who do you think is walking by your picture now?" she would ask Mike out of the blue. "The mayor of New York, I know it. I can feel it."

"Kelly, you're overdoing this," Mike told her, but secretly he loved her enthusiasm.

"I am not. You know what people are saying: 'This kid is great. He's the Picasso of photography.'" Kelly praised Mike constantly about his schoolwork, his camerawork, his clean room. In many ways Kelly was his mother. She showed up when the band played; she helped him with his homework; she packed his lunch or ironed a shirt if he needed it in a hurry.

Kelly was five years older than Mike and had protected him from much of his parents' craziness until she left for school. For the first time, Mike had to fend for himself. He had no one to tell him it was clear to bring home a friend or to shield him from his mother when she had been drinking.

"What have you been working on while I've been gone?" Kelly asked.

"Not much. I haven't had a lot of time."

"Come on," Kelly urged, but Mike didn't budge from the kitchen.

Mike had always been anxious to show Kelly his latest photographs. She knew something was wrong. "Well?" she questioned.

"Mom spilled out my developing chemicals. One at a time. Just like this. She was angry because I

was in the darkroom instead of in the garage washing the car. I told her the car would be clean before she and Dad were ready to go out, but she wanted it done immediately."

"Oh, no. She promised me," Kelly sighed.

"Promised what?"

"That she would leave you alone."

"Ha!" Mike laughed, but hurt darkened in his eyes. "I hate it here without you, but it's not as bad as it was in the beginning." Mike did not explain why.

The next morning Kelly answered the phone and spoke with Will Taylor, a friend of Mike's. "But, Mike told me there was no band practice. What do you mean he hasn't been for weeks?"

"Lots of weeks," Will told Kelly reluctantly. "Mr. Eden said that if Mike doesn't start coming to practice he can consider himself out."

"Thanks for calling, Will. I'll give Mike the message." Kelly hung up, took paper and pencil to write down the chemical names, and went downstairs to Mike's darkroom. She planned to replace the chemicals as a surprise. She turned on the light.

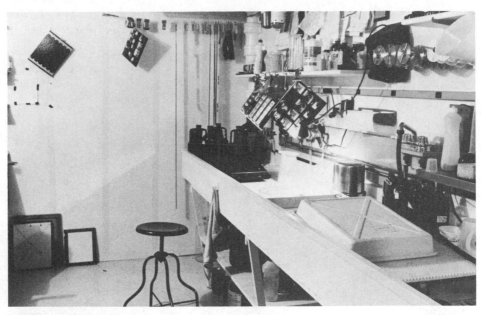

She recognized the hanging photos instantly. There was Kelly swimming, hugging a friend, packing her room for college. No unprocessed rolls of film lined the counter. The once spotless developing trays had layers of dust. Mike had not been in his darkroom since she left. No band practice. No new pictures. Kelly was piecing these

discoveries together when
the doorbell rang. She
grabbed a photo and closed
the door.

"Hi," she greeted a tough-
looking boy she had never
seen before.

"Mike around?"

"He's sleeping. Who are
you?" she asked, not liking
this boy on sight.

"Howie. Howie Astor. I
live on Summit."

"I'll get Mike. Want to
come in?" She was being
polite without meaning to
be.

"I'll wait out here." Howie
sensed Kelly didn't like him.

"Mike, get up. It's after
eleven o'clock. There's some

guy, Howie, here. He's outside. And you and I have to shop for the
party." Kelly poked her brother gently.

"Let Mom shop."

"Come on, Mike. You know better. Mom won't be up 'til three."

Mike felt awful, but he could not say "No" to Kelly. "Okay, okay, I'm getting up."

"What should I tell that Howie person?" Kelly asked.

"Tell him to call me later."

Then Kelly noticed. *"Mike!"* she shrieked. "What's that doing here?" She pointed to an empty beer bottle at the end of the bed. "In Mom's room, yes. In here?" Kelly was hysterical.

Mike buried his head under the pillow. "Get up this minute," Kelly ordered. "Get dressed. Get up, I said. Now." Kelly sent Howie home and tried to calm down while she waited for Mike to dress.

"What's going on? Beer in your room. A kid I never saw at the door. No new pictures. Not one. The roll you took at the end of the summer is still hanging, and Will told me that you haven't been at band practice for weeks. Answer me." Kelly waved the photograph and beer bottle in Mike's face.

Mike didn't know what to say. He peeled his orange and avoided looking at his sister. He wanted to say he was sorry he upset her. He wanted to tell her he didn't know what to do. He wanted to explain that he drank to shut out his mother. He really just wanted to cry.

• • •

When they arrived at the supermarket, Kelly tried again. "Mike, you have to talk to me. You have to tell me what's going on." Mike looked away, and Kelly turned the cart and went in to shop.

Inside Mike stayed silent. He tailed along, twisted the shopping list, and stared at the crumpled page. Kelly kept asking until Mike finally blurted out everything. "It's all true. No band. No pictures. Mom did throw out my chemicals. That really happened. Lots of beer. I dropped photography club. And wait 'til you see my grades.

"I tried. I wanted to get A's like you, but I can't study. Mom's either banging around laughing or banging around crying and slamming doors. Dad comes home and he starts. You know."

"Sure, I know, Mike."

"I really tried. I can't be an honor student like you were. I'll never get a scholarship. I don't want one anyway." Mike felt sorry for himself.

"Oh, brother! So you're doing what Mom does. Where do you think drinking will get you?" Kelly wanted to scream, but she didn't dare. "I didn't get my scholarship by copping out. Mom and Dad are who they are. You're you. I'm me. I can't play a clarinet or take a decent picture. You won a national competition over thousands of entries."

"So what? I still can't bring home friends. I can't even develop pictures in the house if Mom's drunk or wants something."

"You are going to do exactly what I did," Kelly instructed her brother quietly and sympathetically as the clerk checked them out. "First, you're going to start studying at the library and you're going to promise me you won't drink."

"I am?" Mike asked.

"You are." Kelly smiled. "It's tempting; there's alcohol in our house. Mom's drunk most of the day, and Dad's drunk almost every night. But there's alcohol in most houses. Will can drink, but he doesn't. Right?"

"That's true," Mike agreed, "but Howie does."

"Dump Howie. You need to join Alateen like I did."

"Those meetings you were always going to?"

"You'll make friends with kids who have the same problems you have. You're not the only one with alcoholic parents. I'll go with you tonight. You'll end up like Mom if you don't. I couldn't stand that. I love you too much." Kelly hugged her brother.

"Kelly, stop it. You're embarrassing me." But Mike liked and needed his sister's love. He was relieved that Kelly knew he was drinking and that she was watching out for him. He would do what she said. He made up his mind to try.

"Do you think Mr. Eden will let me stay in band?"

"He better," Kelly smiled. "What will I do on Saint Patrick's Day if I can't watch you march in the parade?"

You Should Know

1. Alcoholism is an illness like heart disease, cancer, or diabetes. It has nothing to do with willpower. Many alcoholics drink only once a week or once a month. Their drinking, be it occasionally or daily, is painful or harmful to themselves and others. Some stop for a while, then start again. There is no cure for this disease, but a good treatment program can keep the illness from reappearing by teaching drinkers how to stay away from alcohol.

2. Alcoholics Anonymous (AA) is an organization for people who are having trouble controlling their drinking. Meetings are held—at first every day—to discuss problems and to try to find solutions. Members, all of whom once had or still have serious drinking problems, support the efforts of fellow members who want to stop drinking and stay stopped and sober.

3. Alateen, like AA, holds regular meetings for young people who have parents who drink. Meetings present an excellent opportunity to make friends with kids who are faced with similar problems at home. Children of alcoholics, like Kelly and Mike, learn that they are not alone; that there are actions they can take to help keep up grades; and that they can lead happy, fulfilling lives.

4. A child who lives with an alcoholic parent feels alone and isolated, different from his friends. He's constantly on the defensive, never quite sure how the parent is going to act or react. Special counseling and groups such as Alateen are one way teens can live with and understand an alcoholic parent.

5. Alateen and Alcoholics Anonymous have chapters throughout the country. Local chapters are listed in the telephone book under "Alcoholism" or the chapter's individual name.

6. Mike started drinking to avoid the pressures created by alcohol-abusing parents, to cover his bad feelings about his grades not being up to his sister's, and to fill the time once spent talking and joking with Kelly. What Mike didn't know is that children of alcoholics are four times more likely to become alcoholics than children whose parents are not addicted to alcohol.

You can see why Mike and others with alcoholic parents have to be especially careful and need good information about drinking.

7. An alcoholic parent is too in favor of drinking to be able to give sound and honest information about the effects of drugs.

Keep in Mind

1. Parents like Mike's are not the best role models, but a parent does not have to be a steady drinker to send out wrong messages. Any parent who lives on tranquilizers or constantly takes pills when they're not really needed for a medical problem has a drug habit. Just being aware of a parent's drug habit is often enough to keep a child from following that parent's example.

2. Alcohol, marijuana, and other drugs make life *seem* easier for some people. Mike drank too much to block out his parents' horrible drinking behavior. He felt helpless without Kelly and embarrassed about his home life, but drinking only made him feel guilty. He knew deep down that alcohol was not the answer and that his sister would be angry.

3. Big problems—such as living with an alcoholic parent, being in constant battle with a parent, not understanding schoolwork, not having any friends—can't be improved by getting drunk or doped up.

4. The more a person uses drugs to help him get through tough times, the less able he is to deal with them—sober or drunk. In other words, a person who wrongly uses alcohol to wipe out unhappiness will find that the problems disappear only for the moment. They are still there when he sobers up.

5. Mike made his life even more complicated by believing he had to do as well as Kelly had done in school. Mike, like each of us, has his own strengths—a talent for photography and music—to give him good feelings and win him praise. No two people are the same, and trying to live up to someone else's accomplishments can lead only to disappointment.

6. There is always help for problems like Mike's. Most of us need guidance about something, but too few ask. Alateen was Kelly's and would be Mike's source of support and advice. Keep in mind: It's not a sign of weakness or stupidity to find help for whatever is upsetting you.

Chapter 12

You're Responsible

You read the important facts about alcohol and marijuana. You learned how to deal with common pressure situations. But you still may be unsure.

Let's set the record straight. There's a reason so many kids are drinking and appearing to have fun doing it. For some, there's no question that drinking often wins approval from their friends. Are these really the people they want or need for friends? For others, drinking gives them something to do. Still others use alcohol to hide their insecurities . . . temporarily.

For those who use alcohol as the great escape or who keep experimenting, there is a major snag: No one knows who will get hooked or why some people do and why some don't. For those who become addicted, the drug route can only be a "bummer."

Ask any kid—or adult—who has abused alcohol, pot, or other drugs, and he can provide a long list of problems and unpleasant scenes. It will include family fights, school failures, police trouble, endless jams, and health problems. Equally rough, maybe rougher, is recovery. He'll tell you how many times he tried to get straight and failed and how he can never in his whole life touch another drink—not one sip.

If you want to drink, you will find a way no matter what the legal barriers or parental restrictions. But drinking should be something you have considered seriously. Unless you're a hermit, you are going to be confronted one of these days. Don't let someone else decide for you.

Sure, we all care what our friends think of us. Friends are very important. You need them, and they need you, but their opinion is not any better than yours. You and your friends are together because you like the same sports, have the same interests, or share the same hobby, but stop to think.

Do they have the exact same attitude about everything? Suppose your best friend became a cocaine user, would you? Suppose he gave up track, or she gave up dance and it was the activity you loved most. Would you give it up, too? We have many things in common with our friends, but not everything.

If the bonds between you are strong, if friends *really* care about you, it should not make any difference what you do about drinking. If you feel strongly about avoiding alcohol and pot, don't compromise. Be a leader. If you have to, be the only one who doesn't drink. You may be able to get your friends to think your way. Take the chance. You'll feel better about yourself because you did what you believed in, not what "friends" told you or wanted you to do.

The facts are straightforward. People who hide behind alcohol or need it to make them feel good have a serious problem. Growing bodies are not ready to handle quantities of alcohol, nor are young minds mature enough to deal very well with the impulses that alcohol may release.

Who wants to have the whole school discussing the black eye you gave your best friend in last night's brawl? Who wants to be dizzy, nauseated, or seen puking out his guts? Who wants to face his mother with swollen eyes that she's sure to know were not caused by the flu? The hassle of lying to your parents, feeling guilty, getting caught, and getting grounded is rarely worth it.

There are no prizes for drinking. Ever. Especially on the home front. You should know your parents' views on drinking and drugs. Many parents are uncomfortable discussing drinking. Some don't want to enter a discussion they think will end up in a fight; others do not accept the fact that alcohol is a dangerous drug. Bring up the subject if they don't.

Most parents care about their children and want to help if they can. But be prepared for them to have ideas and feelings that are very different from yours. Be ready for them not to believe a word you say. They may want to hear only what they have to say, not what you might want to talk about. The other side is they may know more than you think and be able to answer your questions.

Set up some guidelines at the start of your discussion: Tell them you will speak honestly, but in turn you don't want them to ask questions about who is using or selling drugs. Ask them to agree not to change your curfew and not to get hysterical. You may also want to give them this book to read before you talk.

Pick a time when they're not rushing off to a meeting, racing around preparing dinner, or running water for your sister's bath. A good place to start is by telling them what's going on at your school—how easy it is to buy drugs—and what's happening at parties.

If you're pretty sure your parents are the wrong people to talk to, or if you have tried and they don't listen, there are others who can guide you: a school counselor, a doctor, a social worker, a clergyman, or sometimes a best friend's parent. Look in the phone book for family services in the area. Most hospitals have special alcohol and drug units. Call or stop in to talk with one of the counselors. A family friend or relative might be delighted that you came to her for advice.

Don't be discouraged if the first person you choose is not helpful, makes you feel uncomfortable, and seems to be judging you. Try someone else. There are many, many people who understand what you are up against. Whatever advice others or your parents give you, they cannot be solely or completely responsible for your attitudes and drug habits. They can neither protect you from all bad things nor control you or your decisions.

In spite of what you read, you either may decide to experiment or weaken under the pressure. No one is perfect. If you've had a drink or two or have been bombed out of your mind or stoned out of your head on marijuana, you don't have to keep doing it. If you're feeling guilty, stop. Choose differently next time. You don't have to continue to be the life of the party. When there's another gathering, don't appear. If you go, say, "No, not tonight."

When you're surrounded by beer cans and loud laughter or overwhelmed by marijuana smoke in a friend's basement, if you're thinking "No," say it. Many times saying "No" to your sister when she wants to borrow your makeup or "No" to your brother when he asks to use your bike is an automatic response. Sometimes you say "No" to your family before you hear the whole question. You can just as quickly say "No" to your friends when they want you to drink or drug with them.

Make a pact with yourself. Just say "No." It can be that simple. You won't let yourself down. After all, you're responsible for you.